UNDER *the*
CHINOOK ARCH
Tales of a Montana Veterinarian

BY R. W. "RIB" GUSTAFSON, D.V.M.

Library of Congress Catalog Card Number: 93-90729
ISBN: 1-56044-248-4

Published by R. W. Gustafson, Route 1, Box 136,
Conrad, Montana 59425, in cooperation with
SkyHouse Publishers, an imprint of Falcon® Publishing, Inc.,
Helena, Montana.

Design, typesetting, and other prepress work by
Falcon Graphics, Helena, Montana.

Cover painting by Pat Gustafson.

Distributed by Falcon®Publishing, Inc.,
P.O. Box 1718, Helena, Montana 59624,
phone 1-800-582-2665.

First Printing 1993
Second Printing 1994
Third Printing 1998

Manufactured in the United States of America

CONTENTS

UNDER THE CHINOOK ARCH

ACKNOWLEDGMENTS

I WISH TO GIVE SPECIAL THANKS TO THE PEOPLE WHO helped me make this book a reality—my clients, who made these stories possible; my wife and family, who accompanied and helped me during forty-three years of practice; my daughter Kristen, for typing and proofreading the manuscript; Falcon Press/SkyHouse Publishers and Noelle Sullivan, who encouraged me and aided me in the publishing process; Robert Scriver, for the foreword and constructive ideas; *FARM JOURNAL* and its editor Earl Ainsworth, who purchased my first story and gave me permission to include it in this book; and all those who have said, "Rib, you should write a book."

I offer special thanks to my wife, Pat Gustafson, for her outstanding oil painting of the Chinook Arch used on the cover. I dedicate this book to her and to our family, a family being the basic unit of a good society.

RIB GUSTAFSON

FOREWORD

I WAS PLEASED AND FLATTERED WHEN RIB GUSTAFSON, A respected friend of long standing, asked me to review his manuscript, *Under the Chinook Arch*, made up of tales of his life as a veterinarian in Montana. Feeling inadequate, and with a great deal of trepidation, I summoned up the courage to start. I know very little of his profession, except that whenever I had a sick animal of any breed or species I always called Rib. Not until I had read his manuscript did I realize the depth of his knowledge and the honesty and integrity of the man himself.

His story, as it unfolds, is an amazing collection of excerpts from a most unbelievable career. I had allowed two or three nights to carefully read the manuscript, but once I had started I could not put it down. I finished reading it in one evening! The tales are all true adventures, vividly told in a remarkable, homey, easy-to-read Montana style. One can feel what he felt: the hard physical work, the constant struggle against all the variables of Montana weather, the miracle of birth, the pathos of death, the feeling of elation upon the successful conclusion of an impossible operation, and the sense of triumph against unbelievable odds.

In his writing, Rib has given us a feeling of what it is like to help not only his animal patients but also his many neighbors, earning their everlasting friendship and devotion. His stories renew one's faith in Montana's truly western way of life, inspiring one to become a good neighbor and lend a helping hand in times of need.

The tales have the clear ring of truth. It is fortunate for us that Rib Gustafson has wanted to share his experiences with us; we will all be richer for it. These are stories that had to be written. Thank God they were preserved by a man who had the gift, perseverence, and ability to do just that.

An amazing book by a truly amazing man. Thanks, Rib, from all of us who read *Under the Chinook Arch*.

BOB SCRIVER
BROWNING, MT

vi

Introduction

I REALLY CAN'T PUT MY FINGER ON THE REASON I WANTED to become a veterinarian. I lived on a ranch as a small child, until my father died when I was seven years old. His death left my mother with eight children to raise by herself. I spent the next few summers on my uncle's small ranch near Rapelje, Montana. I loved to ride horses, and my weekly highlight was a horseback trip to see how the cattle were doing. I waited anxiously for the days when my aunt would yell up the stairs, "Uncle Louie said you could ride today." No time was spent dillydallying then. I didn't even have to be pushed to cram down the oatmeal mush that was our usual breakfast fare. All I wanted was to be on the horse and away from the normal drudgery of other chores.

Those were great days. My dog would leap in wild anticipation, and we would be off down the coulee, in a different world for the day. The rapport between a horse and a dog and a boy grew. About three miles down the coulee, a small spring flowed out of a sandstone cliff; I would stop there to get a drink of clear, cold water. Above the spring, in overhanging cliffs, were several old Indian paintings that had to be looked over. While I did that, my dog was in constant pursuit of fat groundhogs that always seemed to elude him. Having surveyed the paintings and animal life, we would proceed on our way to the cattle pasture, accompanied by hawks circling and screeching in the sky over our heads.

My uncle ran between thirty to forty head of cattle in a section of rough land during the summer. I was to count them all. It was a great catastrophe when I found two dead heifers. I loped the horse nearly all the way home to give Uncle Louie the news. He had had a rupture and didn't ride, so we climbed into the old Chandler, an ancient make of car now extinct, and went back to the scene. Lightning had killed them, he said.

Another time, I found a heifer in labor. When my uncle and I returned, we hooked the old Chandler onto the calf's legs and pulled it. The calf was dead, but the heifer lived.

In the summer of 1935 or 1936, an epidemic of sleeping sickness hit our horse herd. First it took old Patty, one of the workhorses. She died quickly. Then Dick, one of the saddle horses, went down. He beat his head on the ground for a week before my uncle finally put him out of his misery.

There were no practicing veterinarians within sixty miles. All treatments for sleeping sickness were hearsay, so I spent some time every day painting the horses' ears with crankcase oil. This was supposed to keep insects that cause sleeping sickness out of their ears. Only one more horse, Fox, showed any symptoms of the disease. He had a mild case and recovered but always remained spooky and goofy. I felt I had played a small part in the treatment and prevention, anyway, even if I had made all the horses head-shy.

One other event impressed me and moved me toward a career in animal health. My uncle had a young stallion to castrate, and he called on an old cowboy to do the job. The horse was thrown and tied with numerous ropes. Wooden clamps were used, and the cords were seared with hot irons. The entire job took nearly half a day, but my uncle gave the man five dollars. Normal wages then were thirty dollars a month, so five dollars for half a day looked to me like a quick trip down easy street.

By the time I finished high school, I began to put veterinary medicine down as my occupational preference. I didn't know how this could ever come about or even what was involved, but it looked quite a bit better than a future as a farm and ranch hand. I took eighty dollars in savings and entered college. I completed two quarters before my money ran out.

World War II ended all future plans for awhile. I enlisted as a naval cadet and served as an aviator until the conflict ended. The GI bill made my desire to become a veterinarian come true. I had given serious thoughts to becoming a regular Navy man, but I turned down a round-the-world cruise on our newest and largest carrier at the time. It meant signing up for two more years of service. The pull of Montana and the way of life I knew looked much better. Besides that, with the money I had saved, I could attend school without undue financial worry.

With two whoops and a holler, and a good drunk to celebrate my separation from the service, I embarked on a career that I would always be happy about.

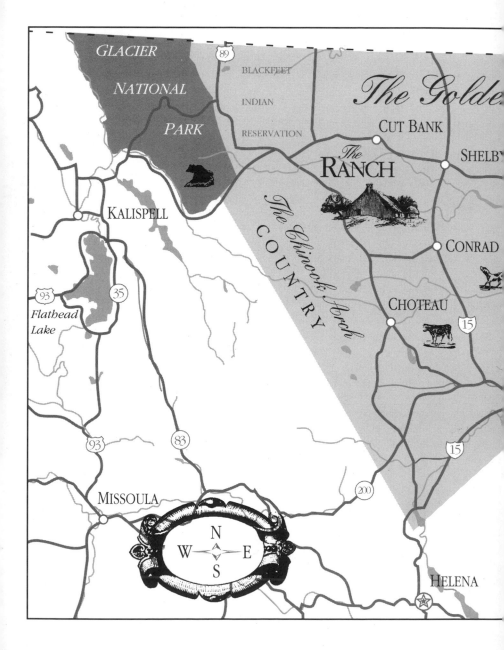

GLACIER

NATIONAL

PARK

89

BLACKFEET

INDIAN

RESERVATION

CUT BANK

The Golde

SHELBY

The
RANCH

KALISPELL

The Chinook Arch
COUNTRY

CONRAD

93

35

CHOTEAU

15

Flathead
Lake

93

83

15

200

MISSOULA

N
W E
S

HELENA

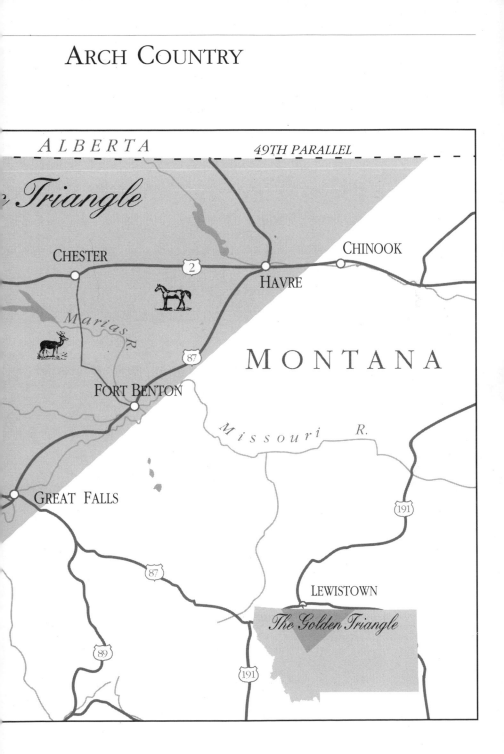

THE FIRST YEARS

THE PRACTICE OF VETERINARY MEDICINE IS MORE THAN A profession. It is a way of life, and a very demanding way of life for a general practitioner in a large, sparsely inhabited area. It is demanding both physically and mentally. This may be the reason it appeals to so many people: life as a veterinarian is never boring. In forty-three years of practice, when I woke up in the morning, I never knew where I would end up in the evening.

As in all things, there is some drudgery. Working cattle through a chute all day long is sometimes tedious, but the fact that a completely different task usually lies ahead makes the job easier. Sometimes working conditions aren't too pleasant, but the people doing the job are. There is always humor. Laughing, happy, friendly people make a long day short or a hard job easier.

The weather also plays an important part. Montana is a land of extremes. Long and bitter cold spells can alter many plans. Conditions can change so rapidly that it would sound like fiction

WITH TWO OF MY GRANDSONS: FUTURE VETERINARIANS.

1

if I were to relate all the experiences I've had. The old saying "If you don't like the weather, wait a few minutes" is oftentimes true.

There is an old saying that goes something like this: "An educated fool is one who learns more and more about less and less until he knows everything about nothing." Looking back, this was probably true in my case. When the professors in school got together and decided that I was ready for practice, little did I realize what they meant. I thought that I knew everything after those strenuous, fun-filled years as a college student. I was going to set the world on fire with all the knowledge I had accumulated. No one ever went out into the world more confident.

As students, we had been crammed full of theories, treatments, diseases, and methods until we were supposed to know it all. If ignorance is bliss, I certainly was full of bliss.

During the first few years, it was hard to admit to myself that an old rancher who knew everything an animal did from the day it was born until the day it died could possibly know more about one than I did. "The master's eye fattens the calf," the Bible says, and that saying today still holds plenty of water for me.

As with good things about veterinary practice, there are also sad things. Death and taxes are inevitable. No one can win all contests, and everyone has to accept a few losses. Losses are not easy, but they do come less often when you really try. I never read any Tennyson, but I think there is an old saying attributed to him that rings true. "It is better to have loved and lost," he wrote, "than never to have loved at all." This holds doubly true if you substitute the word "try" for "love." The old man must have been quite a philosopher.

My wife and family have put up with the uncertainties of a veterinarian's existence, and for this they should be enshrined in a hall of fame somewhere. In a veterinarian's life, the best-made plans sometimes go awry, and the hours spent waiting are innumerable. The number of meals missed is unmentionable. The nights of worry and anxiety, I know, have been trying to my family. God bless them all!

As every young boy has his dreams of the future, so I had mine. Ever since the day on a ranch in the Madison Valley, years ago, when a veterinarian looked into a horse's mouth and told my brother and myself just how old the horse was, I knew what I wanted to do. At first, the thought of becoming a veterinarian was just a shadow I kept seeing until it became an obsession that never left me. My increasing desire to reach this goal finally became a reality about twelve years later, when they handed me a degree as a Doctor of Veterinary Medicine from Colorado Agricultural and Mechanical Arts College (Colorado State University) and a license to practice in the state of Montana.

Forty-three years later, I feel I was not wrong in choosing my ambition. The years have been good, and the experiences of these years are ever increasing joys as I look into the past. The people I have met and worked for leave me with good thoughts toward all people. The satisfaction of contributing to the welfare of all kinds of animals and their proprietors give one a feeling that is difficult to describe in words. Life has never been boring.

FIRST CALL

THE FIRST CHANCE I HAD TO PROVE MYSELF FINALLY
arrived. A rancher on the Marias River was losing cattle and
couldn't seem to put his finger on the cause. The call came
secondhand; the owner of a local tavern where I whiled away my
unemployed hours informed me of the rancher's dilemma. I had
become a very good friend of this bartender because it seemed
no one else knew I was around. I had thought of employing a
secretary to take calls and keep books, but since there were no
calls to take or books to keep, it was much easier to meet friends
at the saloon where most of the people made at least one stop
when they came to town. The owner was happy to relay the call,
I think, since my credit was possibly extended a little too far, and
he probably thought some gainful employment might help
remedy the situation.

The ranch was remote. After several inquiries and many more
miles than necessary, I finally found the right one. The ranch
owner was nowhere around, but his wife supplied me with
coffee and explained that he was out combining grain. I again
searched the ranch to find him, finally, sitting up on the combine
with a mask on his face, amid chaff and dust that made me itch.
He removed the mask, revealing a face more like that of a coal
miner than of a rancher. I informed him of the purpose of my
visit and tried to convince him that he might be able to use my
services.

"Yes," he said. He was losing a few cattle. Seven had died and
a few more were sick. He had never seen anything quite like it
before. And the chance of getting off the combine for a while
must have been pleasurable. We went back to his barn, where he
captured a typical old broomtailed horse. On went the saddle and
the bridle, and he grabbed an old raggy-looking lariat that any
modern-day roper wouldn't be caught dead with.

The cattle were over the hill, which was about four miles from
the house. The rancher loped the horse over in a straight line
while I tried to follow in my car. He was waiting for me after I

4

MY GOOD OLD FRIEND BILL BIG SPRINGS ON THE TRAIL.

had made several detours to avoid coulees, rocks, and sagebrush. I'm sure he had a much easier time than I did.

Anyway, we looked over the cattle and he finally spotted one that was sick. It looked pretty healthy to me. In school all the animals we treated were in small pens with case histories and with the diagnosis and treatments written on cards tacked to the wall. Facilities were readily available to restrain the animal, as were numerous students to supply the labor. Here I was out on the prairie with no diagnosis, no supply of available help, and an animal that I could hardly perceive as unhealthy.

To give myself a little time and to plot what to do next, I visited with the rancher for a while. It wasn't practical to chase the sick critter back to the corrals, I thought. Even if we did get her back there, facilities weren't much better than they were out here in the sagebrush. I procrastinated a little longer by digging through my meager supply of instruments and medicines, wondering what to do when and if we did catch her.

5

Finally, finding no more excuses to prolong the agony, I asked Bob if he would catch her. He tightened up the cinch, uncoiled the old rope that resembled a dishrag, and took off after the heifer. In about twenty seconds the loop settled over her head. He then flipped the rope over her hips, and reined his horse off to the side. That heifer came around and lay down on her side as pretty as any critter in a professional steer-jerking contest. I ran up and grabbed her front leg, slipped on a rope, and tied three legs together. She was captured.

Next came the thermometer and stethoscope, old faithful partners during our years of veterinary school. She had a high temperature, and her heart was pounding like a trip hammer. I threw a few big words around to impress Bob of my medicinal background, words like icterus, dyspepsia, and blood dyscrasia. That didn't help the critter very much, so I gave her an injection of antibiotic, drew some blood from her jugular vein, and turned her loose. That had been fun, so we decided to survey the herd for some more sick cattle. We repeated the process on a couple more and, after a bruised shin and depletion of my medicines, returned to the ranch. I made some slides from the extracted blood, drank another pot of coffee, and with a few indefinite answers as to what was wrong with the cattle departed for town.

With the help of the local hospital, I stained the slides and examined them under a microscope. Sure enough, there as big as life was the culprit: *Anaplasma marginale*, a little bug that gets into the red blood cell and ruptures it. I was elated. The state laboratory confirmed my diagnosis. We returned to the ranch and tested the entire herd. I was on my way in the practice of veterinary medicine. Frank, the bartender, began to see less of me. He also began to spread the rumor that I was passable as a veterinarian, keeping my credit good during that first lean year.

THE FIRST WINTER

MONTANA IS THE LAND OF EXTREMES. OLD MAN WEATHER can make it the most pleasurable place to be, or the most unpleasant. In my first year in the state, for some reason, it started raining in the early fall; by the middle of October, the rain had turned to snow. Roads turned from mud to frozen clods and then to drifts. My services in the country began to diminish as roads became impassable. About the time the snowplows got all the roads plowed, another norther settled in and closed them again. By the first of January we were driving through tunnels in six-foot-high drifts. There was little letup.

About this time, I began to wonder if a large animal practice was economically feasible in this country. With the help of Frank, the local bartender, I began to think of looking at small animals in order to keep my credit good. He agreed to try me out on his own dog . . . maybe he figured that he should get something in return for the drinks and vittles he was supplying.

I had rigged up a makeshift office at the local livestock auction barn. I made a table to examine the pets, purchased a few more instruments to make it look professional, and even put up some shelves to store an increasing supply of drugs. I scrounged an old, used autoclave from a nearby hospital to sterilize instruments and opened the doors for business.

Frank brought his big, old, female Labrador named Mitsy out. I imagine that she had produced about ten litters of pups, judging from the condition of her sagging mammary glands. Frank couldn't find a home for all the mongrel pups she managed to raise. According to him, she always was bred to a good registered hunting lab, but it usually turned out that they grew up to be certified "Heinz 57" varieties. Also, about twice a year, his tavern seemed to collect all the stray dogs from miles around. They would camp outside the door, and with every customer that came in the place, a male companion looking for Mitsy would enter. The time had come to relieve Mitsy of her duties as a mother and to stop the collection of lovers that Mitsy attracted.

Frank was pressed into service as the number-one veterinary assistant, and I proceeded in my attempt to anesthetize Mitsy so the operation could be performed. The larger the dog, the more anesthetic required. Since my supply of syringes consisted of ten cubic centimeter capacity only, one wasn't quite enough to produce the anesthesia required for a spay. After several minutes of thrashing and howling I managed to find the proper vein a second time and get the job done. About that time, I think, Frank began to wonder if it wouldn't have been better to haul the dog ninety miles to the city, where there were veterinarians who specialized in small-animal practice. I convinced him that everything was fine and continued with preparations for the operation.

During my school years, I had convinced myself that I was only going to practice on large animals, so I somehow managed to escape from the educational institution without ever having actually spayed a dog. I had assisted many times, but watching something being done and doing it yourself are two different things. Here I was with my friend and benefactor's dog ready to attempt something that I had never done. I recalled an idiom often repeated in school about never spaying your best friend's dog. I knew then and there that I should have taken advantage of the educational opportunities that had been offered to me.

Frank overcame his premonitions as I prepared myself for the operation. I scrubbed and donned new rubber gloves as he stood over his beloved dog, watching with the intensity of a true dog lover. There was Mitsy, stretched out, draped, and ready to go under the knife.

At the first stroke of the scalpel, a change came over poor Frank. A few drops of blood began to ooze from the incision and the sight of red made him turn as white as a sheet. I inquired if he felt alright. Taking the tough guy approach, he replied, "Don't think a little blood will ever bother me." I proceeded with the operation, twisting small bleeders with the hemostats.

When I looked again, Frank had turned his head away from the scene. About that time, his body began to stiffen, and he fell full length on the floor. The way he went down reminded me of a tall tree falling as the sawyer yells "Timber!" I didn't know whether to go help him or to continue with the operation. Any attention paid to Frank would mean contamination of my sterile state. I recalled some professor mentioning things like this might happen, and that people usually recover from a faint after a few minutes. So I proceeded with the operation while Frank lay there, starry-eyed and stiff.

Having never actually performed the surgery before, I had a few tense moments. I was thankful Frank wasn't standing over me, wondering if he had employed the right veterinarian. I removed and ligated the ovaries and uterine horns and was in the process of closing the incision when Frank came to. "Don't you ever tell anyone about this," he told me.

I assured him that I wouldn't make him the laughingstock of his entire clientele. "Who would ever believe that a big, tough man like you would faint at the sight of a little blood?" I asked.

He packed Mitsy out to his car and left with my instructions to keep her warm and watch so she wouldn't hurt herself when she came out of anesthesia. I began to wonder if I shouldn't have a cage or two in my office in case some client couldn't or wouldn't take care of his own dog when it was recovering from surgery.

Mitsy recovered quickly from the effects of spaying, and Frank never mentioned the fainting episode to anyone. I spayed dogs that winter when I couldn't make it out to ranches during periods of snowbound roads and blizzards. In fact, it was pleasant to spend those cold days indoors instead of fighting roads, putting on chains, and freezing my hands while putting in prolapses or operating on water-bellied calves.

One day, about six months later, I went to pay Frank a visit. Lo and behold! There was Mitsy's amorous crew waiting at the front door for a chance to get next to her. Dogs were all over the place. Evidently I had missed removing part of the ovary or an ovarian cyst at the time of the operation. I couldn't believe it, and a cold chill ran down my spine at the thought of having to go in and meet with Frank's wrath.

I worked up the fortitude to enter, and, sure enough, there was Frank, waiting to give me holy hell. After a few minutes of harangue, I asked him to hold it. "You saw the operation," I reminded him. "You know I removed both the ovaries, don't you?" I could still recall him lying on the floor in a dead faint.

After that I never heard any more about Mitsy's twice-yearly court of suitors, and I never mentioned anything about him fainting at the sight of a little blood until this time.

BRUCELLOSIS

EVEN THOUGH THE FIRST MONTANA WINTER WAS TOUGH, I managed to pursue a habit acquired during my years of high school and college. I liked to ski! I had broken my leg quite badly during my last year of veterinary school and had missed an entire year of the sport, getting through the season without even getting on the boards. With all the snow around and a good ski resort nearby, why not enjoy myself? I wasn't busy enough that winter for anyone to miss me, anyway. When the roads were closed, I could jump on the train and, after a few cocktails, be on the hill.

No one enjoys skiing, especially deep-snow skiing, more than I. At that time, when skiers were few in number, we had miles and miles of untracked snow. Winters would be too short in this paradise, I thought. My weekends were full.

One day after a strenuous session on the hill, I came home with an aching neck and arms and a slight pain in the chest. During the night, the chest pains increased to the point where it was too painful for me to lie in bed. When I got up and moved around, most of the pain went away. I was up and down all night—mostly up, because I felt better that way. I tried to remember what I had hit or when I had fallen while skiing to bring on the pain. I couldn't recall hitting anything hard.

Then it hit me. I recalled having shoved my hand onto a syringe loaded with live vaccine in the office two to three weeks previously. That accident had left a big red sore that refused to heal. I spent a miserable night, and could hardly wait for my friend, Doc Norden, to open his office in the morning.

"Yes, I agree with you," he said. "You have all the symptoms of brucellosis." It wasn't a pleasant thought. It is an occupational hazard of most large-animal practitioners to contract the disease, known as undulant fever in human medicine. I asked if there were any methods of treatment, and he informed me that I was supposed to know more about brucellosis than he.

When a cow gets brucellosis, it is a very serious problem. It is

MUSICIAN AND SON ON THE DAY I LOST A FINGER, 1954.

recorded in the annals of veterinary medicine that there is no cure. Consequently, the U.S. Department of Agriculture has passed rules and regulations on the disease that would stretch from here to the moon. U.S.D.A. staff researchers and state officials must spend half of their time concocting new methods of treating the disease, and even more time writing about it. There is no end to the amount of time and energy that is put into finding a cure or way of controlling it.

I can recall one other tale about the brucellosis problem from that first year. After listening to four hours of discussion about the disease, a veterinarian who was quite short of temper and patience stood up and gave us this analogy:

Brucellosis is classified as a venereal disease in cattle. Any old cow that is found to have it is weighted down with ear tags, branded on the jaw with a big "B," and has a string of papers a mile long that accompany her to slaughter, where the rules say she must go. However, any old prostitute in San Francisco with a known history of gonorrhea and syphilis can climb on a plane and head east without one quarantine paper on her. Her first stop might be Denver, where she lays over a few days to look over the country and spread a few favors. She not only spreads her favors, but also many new cases of V.D. Having viewed all the scenery around the Mile-High City, she takes off for Chicago, where she stops to visit a few friends and, as a sideline, spreads around a few more cases of V.D. After that, she boards the plane for New York City, to continue working seriously at her profession. Now, why didn't she have an ear full of tags, a handful of quarantine papers, and some mark to brand her as a hazard to public health? The poor old cow is being discriminated against once again!

I gradually recovered from the effects of the disease and after a few days of self-pity and unemployment went back to work. There were no clauses for sick leave or unemployment in a veterinary practitioner's contract at that time . . . at least not in mine. It isn't as easy to be sick when you're not getting paid for it. Besides that, my ski trips had depleted my finances and the bank balance wasn't good. Bankers hated losers, and if I didn't get busy, that's just what I would be.

THE FIRST CAESAREAN SECTION

AROUND MARCH 1 OF EVERY YEAR, NEW LIFE BEGINS TO appear in the livestock business, in the form of newborn calves. Even though the work of calving is hard and the hours long, I don't know of a veterinary practitioner who doesn't relish it. There is nothing more satisfying to the soul than bringing into the world a calf from its dam and starting it on life's journey.

The calves come in all sizes, shapes and colors. Their response to the mother is instantaneous, a few tender licks usually bringing out the first weak bellow. Then there is the first attempt to rise. After a few unsuccessful tries, the little calf stands on wobbly legs and takes its first step in search of nutrition. The instincts that lead calves to the proper source are tremendous. In a matter of minutes, they find the nipple sprouting from the mammary glands and ingest the colostrum that gives them instant vigor. One good suckle and a little calf will follow its mother for miles. Calves can also withstand extreme temperatures. I've seen several born in temperatures of twenty-five to thirty degrees below zero. Mother Nature is quite an old girl, but she certainly takes care of her children.

There is also the sad part of the season. In all animals, troubles accompany parturition. Most cases have to do with an oversized fetus. Most first-calf heifers need some assistance in birth. This is given usually by the owner, who keeps them under constant surveillance. The experienced husbandman usually can tell within minutes when help is needed; it is then that the veterinarian rushes to the scene. Night or day, rain or shine, mud or snow, all elements are braved. Sixty- to eighty-mile trips, one way, are not uncommon. If both cow and calf are to be saved, time is essential. A client is satisfied with a live calf at midnight, disappointed with a dead one at six o'clock in the morning. "When is Doc going to get here?" are oft-repeated words.

My first calving season in Montana, the winter had been tough. The Indians had predicted it by saying, "Bad winter, white man puts up lots of hay." My job was to save every animal possible. I

THE FIRST CAESAREAN SECTION

BRINGING IN CHILLED CALVES ON A SNOWY DAY.

had been amply educated in school (I thought), but little did I know what was to come. Nothing can compare to a veterinarian's life from March to May in cattle country.

One night at ten o'clock, the phone rang. On the line, Loren, who lived sixty miles from my nice warm bed, informed me that he had a cow that had been in labor for about two hours. He had examined her and couldn't locate the calf's head, and he doubted she could have it by herself. He lived six miles beyond the top of the pass. The road was bad, but he would meet me on the divide with his power wagon. "Could you please hurry?" he asked.

"O.K.," I'd answered. "I'm on my way."

Snow was falling and wind was picking up when I reached the first foothills. The road began to get narrower, the snowdrifts deeper. More snow flew over the windshield at each new drift, and I finally sighted two dim yellow lights through the snowy haze. The air was pretty fuzzy as I packed my instrument case and a calf-puller into Loren's old World War II-vintage power wagon. If it had a heater in it, I certainly couldn't feel it. I can truthfully say that I wasn't suffering from perspiration for the last six miles of the trip.

We arrived at the barn, where Mrs. Loren was waiting patiently with the kerosene lantern and the proverbial hot water. A quick examination proved Loren right—even I couldn't find the calf's head. It was doubled up in the mother's uterus, so I decided to do my first caesarean section. About that time I found out that Loren was minus one arm, on which hung a prosthetic. Even so, he and his wife were able assistants, and after giving the cow an anesthetic we had little trouble restraining her. I assumed they had worked together for many years as a team, she supplying the extra arm to replace his lost one. They eagerly watched as I shaved the hair off the large abdomen. A flashlight was provided to light my operating area. They never missed a movement, and gave a sigh of relief and joy as a huge calf was pulled from the dam's turgid uterus. The calf took his first gasp of the cold, fresh air and began to look around at his new surroundings as I proceeded to sew up the many layers of the incisions. All went well, and I was amazed at my first success.

By the time we had finished the entire operation, the calf was up and looking for a faucet. He soon found it, and we packed all the equipment and went into the house for the usual coffee and cake. Nothing feels better than an old wood range when coming in from out of the cold; those nice new electric ranges look like refrigerators and feel like them, too, in comparison.

Yes, the Lorens had heard there was a new vet in the country and thought they would give me a try. They sometimes had shot a cow to put her out of her misery in cases like this. They had lived here in the mountains for twenty-five years, and their children were all gone. They didn't know that you could do a caesarean section on a cow. All of us hoped it would be a successful venture.

The trip back home was uneventful, just sixty miles of driving, as the moon made a sporadic appearance between breaking clouds. Jackrabbits darted back and forth on the road, blinded by headlights, then escaped to the deep snow on the prairie, just in the nick of time. Western music from the all-night station pierced my ears to keep me from falling asleep.

Everything went fine for the next couple of days. Business was picking up, and both days and nights were occupied. Just as I was sitting down to the supper that I had prepared in my bachelor's apartment, the phone rang. This time it was Mrs. Loren's voice. She had examined the cow and the sutures seemed to be coming apart. Would I please come back and check? After a few quick bites and a gulp of milk to wash it down, I was on my way again. The roads were better and I made it all the way to the ranch. I racked my brain as to what had gone wrong.

Loren and his wife were waiting when I arrived with the cow tied to the barn wall. The beam from the flashlight showed a gaping incision with the loose end of string hanging from it. Oh, my God . . . the final knot had come untied! What was that about always tying a square knot? In my haste and ignorance I must have given the wrong twist in the suture and ended up with a granny knot. Oh, well. It had cost me a hundred-and-twenty-mile drive, but never again did I end up with a granny knot instead of a square knot.

ALIVE AT ELEVEN, DEAD AT SEVEN

MOST PEOPLE ARE THOUGHTFUL AND KIND. SOME ARE KIND but not thoughtful. Some are neither. Among these are the several clients I've had over the years who know the best time to reach the veterinarian is between five and six in the morning when he is still in bed.

One of these was a man by the name of Russell. My good wife detested this man for two reasons. The first reason was that he was a whiner and complainer; the second was that he made unnecessary phone calls, always in the very early morning hours, often disrupting the physical act of conjugal bliss. He must have had some sort of extra-sensory perception, because his timing was always wrong. If I ever put in an unlisted phone number, it will be because of people like Russell.

However, I never left the phone off the hook or intentionally let it go unanswered. My philosophy was, and always will be, that as a veterinarian I should be available for emergencies

HALF MY LIFE HAS BEEN SPENT ON THE PHONE.

18

anytime, day or night. In fact, I often had to encourage some too-thoughtful clients to call when necessary in emergencies. It is better for both the client and the veterinarian to deliver a live calf at eleven o'clock at night than a dead one at seven o'clock the next morning.

My general rule of thumb is that if a cow in extreme labor does not have a calf within thirty or forty minutes, she needs assistance, either in the form of manipulation and gentle traction or in the form of caesarean-section surgery. A calf will usually live from two to four hours after the onset of labor. This gave me time to drive as far as one hundred miles and still arrive in time to deliver a live calf. In some cases where the owner or his employee has applied undue traction or rough aseptic manipulation, the life span in utero is much shorter. So my advice was, "Don't do anything rash, and I'll be there as soon as possible!"

On arrival, my first action was a quick physical examination of the cow and fetus. The presentation had to be proper: either anterior with the forelegs and head presenting themselves simultaneously, or breach with the rear legs coming first. There are so many variations of this that I'm certain this is the reason our mentors have kept lengthening the term of our education in order to cover all the possible positions in obstetric cases. The first cause of dystocia in all animals is a fetus too large to pass through the pelvic canal. The second is malpresentation in the form of a leg or legs malpositioned.

Whenever I feel two front feet the size of a normal yearling that fill the entire pelvic area, radical surgery in the form of a caesarean section is indicated. I always give the owner the prerequisite of applying the Chinese doctrine "Double or nothing!" and start the operation.

It takes very little time to anesthetize an animal, restrain it, and prepare the surgical site. My favorite is the ventral midline operation that I feel comfortable with and have performed over the many years of practice. In about five minutes I can usually have a live calf out and struggling to stand. By the time I've sutured several layers of tissues, the neonatal calf is nosing around looking for the faucet of life. It gives one a very good feeling to see and hear signs of contentment from both cow and calf during the first nursing. The tail of the little newborn wiggles from side to side, and the nuzzling of the dam seals the bonding.

There are a few ranch managers in our country who know exactly when to call the veterinarian, night or day. One in particular tickles me. He always tells his employees to be very clean and gentle when examining the cow during calving and to always keep a pocketful of change.

"Why the pocket full of change?" they ask.

"So in case there is trouble or doubt, you can rush to the phone and call your friendly veterinarian," he replies!

CHINESE DOCTOR

MY FRIEND BOB VENTURED INTO THE CATTLE BUSINESS after returning from duty as a Navy pilot in World War II. He put all his savings, plus every cent he could borrow from the bank, into a sizeable herd of cattle. But a drop in the beef market left him strapped financially. Returns from his calf sales did not cover his operating costs and bank debt.

One night Bob called me out of a warm bed to tell me he had not one but two heifers that could not have their calves without help. I arrived at his place as soon as possible. The two heifers were in labor in a rickety old shed, five miles from any modern conveniences. No electricity. No warm water. The temperature was about zero.

I roped one heifer and examined her. Her pelvic capacity was small, and the calf was enormous. There was no way it could be delivered through the normal channel. I told Bob the best method to save it would be by caesarean section.

"How much does that cost?" he asked.

I told him thirty-five dollars.

He winced. He had heard that it was possible to do c-sections on cattle, but his belief in a positive outcome was lacking. He pictured two dead cows and a bill for seventy dollars that he didn't have.

I convinced him we had better try.

He seemed as worried about the bill as he was about the surgery's success. "I'll tell you," he said. "Chinese doctors have a different way of going about this. When they work on patients, they don't receive anything unless the patient lives. If the patient dies, they get nothing. If he lives, they get double. Double or nothing, is that a deal?" he asked.

I thought for a moment, then an idea came to me. Since there were two heifers, why not take one of the heifers in payment? I was willing to gamble if he was. We made a deal. I was to receive one-half of the survivors. He wouldn't have to pay one cent in cold, hard cash.

Conditions in the surgical room left much to be desired. I wished for sky hooks as we tied the animal down. We used the headlights of my car and a flashlight that worked sporadically. I had warm water with me, but by the time we finished the first operation, the instruments, needles, and suture were a frozen mass on the tray. We had one live, chilly calf, however. And the heifer was back on her feet.

I put the instrument tray under the car's heater, and we caught the second heifer. She had a calf coming backward, with its hind legs dislodged in a forward position. Her pelvic cavity was narrower than the other heifer's. I attempted unsuccessfully to right the position of the fetus while trying to find out if it was still alive. Standing nearly stripped to the waist in zero-degree weather takes some of the enjoyment out of delivering calves.

After giving the cow a spinal anesthetic, we tied her down. By that time, the instruments were warm and free of ice. We replaced the instrument tray with the chilly first-born calf and proceeded with the second operation.

It doesn't take long to make an incision through a cow's belly wall and uterus. In a few minutes, we had another squirming, blinking calf lying by his mother's side. I didn't envy his abrupt entry into the cold world after spending nine months in the warmth of his mother's uterus.

I began the slow, tedious job of repairing the gaping incisions on his mother. I didn't envy her, either. By the time we had finished, the little calf was staggering to his feet. In doing so, he scattered my instruments and tray all over the barn. I've seen thousands of newborns, but I'm always amazed at their remarkable resiliency.

After picking up the instruments, ropes, and medicines, we found the first-born calf standing up on the front seat of my car, searching for nutrition he knew couldn't be far away. With a few swallows of milk, he would be on his way. I didn't mind the mess he had made. The saying, "They smell better when you own them," started to ring true to my ears.

The first calf suckled while the second dried under the warm air of the car heater. Soon we turned the second one loose. In a few moments, he was making the smacking, slurping sounds of a contented nursing calf.

What a night it had been! A few missing hours of sleep and the stinging pain of numbed fingers couldn't lessen the satisfaction of the sight before me: two little calves being tenderly watched over by their mothers. I felt I had played a small part in the appealing scene.

Bob quickly spread the word about our "Chinese doctor" deal. No one would have to pay for a dead cow . . . Doc would take half the cow for his fee. I ended up with seventeen half-cows. And only once did a client try to renege on his deal.

When prices went up, the offer was still good. But it wasn't long before clients began to pay the going fee.

Is It To Be Fed?

"WAITING FOR A CHINOOK," OR "THE LAST OF FIVE THOUSAND"

WAITING FOR A CHINOOK, BY CHARLES M. RUSSELL. MONTANA STOCKGROWERS'
ASSOCIATION, COURTESY MONTANA HISTORICAL SOCIETY.

MONTANA WEATHER WAS MADE FAMOUS BY ONE SINGLE
picture. In response to an inquiry from an investor, Charlie
Russell sketched a single drooped-horn cow with all of her ribs
showing and enough hip bones protruding to replace a hat rack
and sent it to his boss in response to his questions about the
condition of his cattle. Russell labeled the picture, "Waiting for a
Chinook."

Cattle had been trailed into Montana to feed on the grasses
that previously had been foraged by massive herds of buffalo,
which had roamed since time immemorial. By 1885, the buffalo
were gone, though, and immense herds of cattle were trailed into
Montana from Texas and the Oregon territory to utilize the
renewable resource of grasses and other flora.

Is It To Be Fed?

Russell's picture came from the winter of 1886-1887. The fall months of 1886 had been severe. The snow lay deep, the temperature stayed cold, and northern storms swept down from the Arctic. In January of 1887, chinook winds flowed down the face of the great Rocky Mountains and warmed the country with a rise in temperature of 5.5 degrees for every thousand-foot drop in elevation, bringing the temperature up to around 60 degrees for nearly a week. The snow settled and started to melt. But old "Cold Maker," as the Indians call an arctic air mass, returned and drove the warm air away. The entire melted area was turned into a sheet of ice nearly a foot deep, covering all available forage.

That winter, cattle died by the thousands from "hollow belly," a term used to this day to describe malnutrition. Adding to the starvation was more and more snow, along with extremely cold weather, to add insult to injury. I guess that was Mother Nature's method of maintaining the balance of food available for livestock consumption.

Today, we have a great bureaucracy, nearly one bureaucrat for every livestock producer, to educate people in the livestock industry in how to balance consumption and forage for optimum production. This bureaucracy still has not been able to control the weather, any better than it can make water run uphill. Some of these instant experts think they can walk on water, though, judging by the verbiage they sling around.

The weather still has its way. Droughts come and go, regardless of cloud seeding and iodine crystals. I have seen more snow fall in August than in an entire year. As a veterinarian, I've worked in shirt-sleeves the entire month of January and have seen a total of five feet of snow fall from April 15 to May 15. I've experienced temperature changes from thirty degrees below zero to fifty degrees above within ten minutes. These may seem like tall tales to a "pilgrim" in this country, but we do have records to prove them. You might call me a liar, but any native son will back me. The old saying, "If you don't like Montana weather, wait five minutes and it will change," can certainly be true.

The weather influences veterinary medicine, to be sure. Every month I make a report to the livestock sanitary board on cattle losses from varying diseases to lightning strikes and malnutrition. As a joke, I've sometimes put down an estimate of "hollow belly," whether it be due to plain lack of feed or poor quality feed, sometimes referred to as "wind belly" or "straw belly." It was about three years before the sage group of livestock specialists in Helena who tell us how to run things from behind a desk in a nice warm office took me seriously and started reporting my findings. They report it as malnutrition, however, a word similar to one I coined when I had five kids going to college at the same time. I suffered from "maltuition," then, and it left me and my good wife with a feeling of "hollow belly" at times.

Getting back to the subject of veterinary practice, I was called to a small ranch during a long and severe siege of traditional Montana winter. The ranch owner was a combination farmer, politician, and military general. He had instructed his manager to pen the cattle so they wouldn't exercise too much and to ration their hay consumption to thirteen pounds of hay a day. This ration he had worked out with an old-time county agent who had graduated with him from the agricultural college about thirty years too soon—before they calculated rations according to size, age, weather, and many other factors such as breed, weight, stage of pregnancy, and quality of feed.

The local county agent, who had the nickname "Bromo Pete," relayed the call to me and asked if he could accompany me on the visit to make certain I didn't arrive at a mistaken diagnosis. He had been used for such work before my arrival in the area, instead of the veterinarian, who was not available or had to be brought in at great expense. I told him it would be fine for him to come along, and I picked him up at the drug store. On the ride, drops of foam kept oozing out of the corners of his mouth from the Bromo Seltzer he had just consumed to combat a daily hangover from alcohol consumption, overeating, and chain smoking.

Pete and I exchanged a few pleasantries and humorous stories during our drive to the client's ranch. When we arrived, it was

26

cold and snowy, and the cattle were standing around all humped up. Some of them looked liked they could have replaced Charlie Russell's sketch of "Waiting for a Chinook," or "The Last of the Five Thousand," as someone has dubbed the picture.

The worst to suffer were the three-year-old heifers and a few very old cows that had run out of teeth, whom I often refer to as "golden oldies." The men at the local livestock yard have put a more politically correct name on them, referring to them as "short-term cows." This is more sophisticated, and I've seen many buyers purchase these animals not knowing what the term even means. The buyers can usually relate to me, though, when I refer to the old gals as "plumb gum," meaning they have completely run out of teeth due to advanced age.

As cold as it was that particular day, "Bromo Pete" returned to the car while the foreman and I finished inspecting the cattle and the feed. The cows had nearly depleted all available feed, and the hired men had been digging feed out of the alleyway and throwing it in the mangers in lieu of good alfalfa or grass. I gathered up a good amount of this material, placed it in a sack, and instructed the foreman that drastic measures had to be taken to prevent further losses. He agreed with me, and I concluded my call and returned to the car where "Bromo Pete" was waiting for me to take him back to town and get a nice hot toddy to warm his frigid torso.

I accompanied Pete into the bar when we arrived, and took my sample sack with me to show him what they were feeding the cattle. As Pete was warming up with a hot buttered rum, I dug a handful of feed material out of the sample sack and laid it on a beer serving tray. Pete had warmed up considerably, and he bent over and first smelled the sample. He then rubbed a little of the gooey stuff between his fingers. I knew his sense of humor had returned when he finally turned to me and asked, "Is it to be fed, or has it been fed?"

THE FLYING VETERINARIAN

I ALREADY HAD TWO EXPENSIVE HOBBIES. SKIING USED UP most of my available finances during the winter, and after the first lucky win at a rodeo, I found that summer also could be quite costly. That wasn't enough, apparently. One day a friend commented that I could get around much better if I had an airplane. Expensive hobby number three.

Onno was the friend's name. He had located an airplane and wanted to know if I was interested in becoming his partner. It wasn't hard to convince myself that I could really use a plane. I had visions of flying all over the country instead of putting in long, tedious hours behind the steering wheel of a car. Besides that, the airplane seemed cheap. It would only cost six hundred dollars total, and my share would be just three hundred dollars. Nobody could find a better deal on wings. I said yes, and was on my way to becoming an airborne veterinarian.

I inquired as to the condition of the engine. "Oh, the pistons slap a little," Onno said. "It takes a little oil, but other than that, it runs fine. It has three hundred hours to go before it needs a major overhaul. Besides, it isn't costing you anything to start with." It didn't take much more salesmanship before Onno and I were the proud new owners of an Aer-coupe. The plane could hold two passengers, and had a sixty-five horsepower engine and tricycle landing gear. It was a low-winged mono plane. I could hardly wait to get in and give it a trial spin.

The local airstrips were not overly well-kept, and during a little practice taxiing, I dropped the nose wheel into a gopher hole, tipping the prop. Since Onno didn't fly, I deemed it my responsibility for the catastrophe and forked over sixty-five dollars for a new prop. We were actually supposed to tear down the entire engine, but since it was such a minor thing the mechanic said he would let it go. That wasn't too bad. Only sixty-five bucks before we ever got it off the ground.

I had flown before, but my license had lapsed. Before I could take any passengers, I would have to renew my license. I think business was a little slow around the airport, because the price that a flight instructor charged per hour was twice as much as a veterinarian received. I guess the instructor figured I put in many more hours and could better afford it. I did take one check ride however, applied for a student certificate, and was airborne.

Talk about eating oil. That little old sixty-five horsepower motor could go through a couple of quarts an hour. It damn near broke me up in business to keep the oil tank full. Besides that, I was always looking for a place to land in case the pressure dropped off too much. I got so I could set the thing down on any narrow country road in a crosswind, anytime. The plane's average airspeed was seventy to eighty miles an hour, so unless I cut across country, I didn't save much time in flight. If I hit a headwind, I might as well have stayed home.

In my country, where roads are straight, one doesn't save much time with a plane. By the time I drove to the airport and checked everything out for takeoff, I could have been to wherever I was going. But the romance of flying kept me in the air.

Onno took flying lessons. Between the two of us, we poured all of our spare cash into keeping our little bird airborne. A romantic episode at the time used up most of our hours before we needed a major overhaul. I don't know why girls so far away from home were more interesting than those nearby, but they just were. That, along with the added financing required by the plane, hit the old pocketbook hard. Plus, anyone owning a plane was supposed to be the last of the big-time spenders. I was required to live up to the fame. The vicious circle had captured me: work hard, live fast.

One summer day, a hailstorm came along and put a few dents in the fabric of our precious plane. It didn't seem to bother our plane's performance in the air very much. We painted the fabric with dope, but the climate . . . and an inspector . . . finally took their toll. Cracks and holes began to appear from the sun and wind. The inspector came along with an apparatus to test fabric strength. He not only tested it, but also put several more holes in it. Then he tied a big red notice on it, saying that it was finally unfit for flying because of the fabric. Little did he know of the other defects! A new fabric job would cost more than the plane was worth. After a consultation, Onno and I decided to sell the plane for what we had paid for it. That ended our flying.

Besides, the girls closer to home were beginning to look better and seem more interesting.

DIAGNOSIS

PREGNANCY TESTING AT THE IX RANCH, BIG SANDY.

IT'S TOUGH TO BE A HARD-HEADED SWEDE, WHICH I am. It's even tougher to be a hard-headed Dutchman, by which name I collectively allude to everyone who isn't a Swede.

Slim was a heavy-drinking Dutchman, a wheat farmer with several children and many bad habits, the worst of which was an alcoholic tendency. He was honest enough to call himself a periodic alcoholic. I don't know what the true definition of a periodic alcoholic is. By observing Slim, I think it means to tie on a good drunk every weekend, then spend the rest of the week postponing a hangover by sobering up on beer. Like most alcoholics, he was always broke. But Slim also liked to gamble, which in his case was almost as expensive and addictive as alcohol.

Somewhere along the line he had purchased a milk cow to keep milk and butter on his table and expenses down at home. One day he called to ask if I would stop by and check old Bess. Her bag was beginning to swell, he said, and he thought she could be getting mastitis. Nothing like this had happened to her before, since she had been milked continuously for two years.

"No big rush," he said. "Just stop by when you are somewhere in the area so I don't have to pay for a special call."

I happened to pass by his place a few days later and dropped in to see what was wrong with the animal. I found only two small children at home. They willingly directed me to the cow, who was contentedly munching on hay. She appeared perfectly happy. I put her in the milking stall for a closer examination. Her temperature was normal. A close exam of the mammary glands

31

showed no trace of mastitis or infection. The glands were beginning to enlarge, however, and there was a slight amount of edema just anterior to the glands, a condition often associated with advancing pregnancy.

In order to give the cow a rest before parturition, I told the children to tell Slim to stop milking her. "He never milks her," the older toddler said. "My brothers or sister always milk her." I told them the reason for the order and they were ecstatic knowing that there was to be a new addition to the bovine population of the farm. I left feeling that there had been no need for Slim's call in the first place, and was wondering why it had been made.

The next morning on his daily trip to town, Slim caught me at the office and tore into me with a verbal barrage that would make a muleskinner blush. I was no good as a vet and didn't know anything, he said. My diagnosis was wrong, and for all of his concern, I might as well leave the country. He asserted that the cow could not be with calf. He lived twenty miles from the next herd of cattle, and the cow had never been off his place. He swore there was no way that she could have been bred. All of his speech was sprinkled with copious amounts of profanity.

I hadn't actually tested the cow for pregnancy, but during my examination I was certain I detected fetal movement. It wasn't too easy to stand there and take the humiliating remarks thrown at me. My pride was hurt, and my temper was beginning to run a little short. I was hard-headed enough to stick with my diagnosis, knowing, however, that his statement about her proximity to a source of conception was true. There were no bulls within twenty miles of his farm, and no one was available to artificially inseminate the cow in the entire area.

There we stood, at loggerheads. Slim finally broke the ice, proposing a solution. "I'll bet you fifty dollars she isn't pregnant," he offered. This offer I readily accepted, and we both parted with satisfaction. I still knew I was right, and Slim, confident that he was betting on a cinch, departed for the local tavern to spend the newly earned revenue in his usual manner. I went about my business, hoping I could teach him a lesson for not accepting the diagnosis I had made.

About two weeks later, while passing in the vicinity of Slim's home, I decided to check on Slim's milk cow myself and to possibly collect my winnings. A shadow of doubt had crept into my mind with the passage of time; I wanted to make certain that I could not have been wrong.

I drove into the yard at the farmstead and was again greeted by the two preschoolers. They followed me to the pen where old Bess was still standing at the feed bunk eating away. Her udder was huge, but there was no sign of a new calf anywhere. I made a quick check and found no evidence of any infection. The edema was gone, and her belly had diminished in size.

I asked the children what happened to her calf. "Oh, Daddy took it away and sold it the day after it was born," one child informed me. "He said we needed all the milk."

"We promised to take care of it but Daddy still took it away," the other said. "Someday we hope he lets us keep one."

"I hope he does too," I replied, and left.

As I drove through the wheat fields, I still wondered where old Bess had found a bull. I know that cows in heat become restless and search for male companionship. It may be that she traveled miles one night to find a mate, or maybe they met halfway. Maybe it was a divine conception. I have a hunch that Mother Nature and instinct sent that cow to the proper place. I'll never know for certain, since animals can't talk . . . and what weird tales they would tell if they could.

I sent Slim a little note with his monthly statement, mentioning the fifty dollars. I hoped he wouldn't whip his kids for spilling the beans. His neighbors said that he wouldn't do that, and they also informed me that the children were well fed and well clothed, so my conscience didn't bother me about that.

Slim finally came around and paid off the wager. He apologized for his behavior, and we parted on more cordial terms than after our first meeting. His life seemed to get better, too. Eventually, he quit drinking up the farm, and his kids were able to keep the next calf that arrived . . . via artificial insemination.

Uterine Prolapse

IT IS QUITE COMMON FOR A COW IN HER GREAT POWERS OF labor during parturition to also push out her own entire uterus. The bovine species has a cotyledonous-type uterus that, for some reason or another, is more disposed to prolapse than that of any other species. The calf's first bed, which has held a sixty- to one hundred-pound fetus, is an enormous organ. Once it is completely everted and outside of the animal there is no way it can return to normal without help. The cow has a tendency to remain in labor with this huge organ hanging out, making it extremely difficult to replace unless proper medication is given to quiet her muscles. To put it mildly, uterine prolapse is a spectacular catastrophe that needs immediate attention if the life of the animal is to be saved.

It usually occurs in first-calf heifers after a prolonged and difficult labor. In most cases, the uterus is expelled by an additional labor contraction seconds after birth. The cow may or may not be able to get up with her uterus hanging down to her hocks. If she does rise, it doesn't take her long to find out things aren't normal. Often, she will lie down and await her inevitable end unless the condition is corrected.

I've had to treat more than one case of prolapse. One that I remember was for a local called Old Jim. Jim was a typical "flashlight farmer." He and his wife ran a store and post office during the day and had a few hundred acres of wheat land that he farmed in the wee hours of the mornings and evenings. On top of all that, he had a sizable herd of registered cows that he took care of as best he could any time of the day or night.

As he was making the last check of his cows just before dark one night, Jim found a prolapsed heifer lying on the prairie five miles from the nearest corrals. As oftentimes happened, the rural phones didn't work, or the line was busy when it was really needed. So Jim drove twenty miles into town and caught me as I was just getting ready for bed. He stuttered a little, but after a prolonged discussion, I ascertained what the problem was.

Uterine Prolapse

Trailing cattle under the Chinook Arch.

I loaded up five gallons of hot water and followed him out to the scene, arriving with a car sounding like a hot rodder's after losing a muffler in a battle with the boulders on the untracked prairie. It was cold and dark. The temperature was about zero, but a brisk wind hit me in the face, making it feel like twenty below. The cow was still alive. Jim said it looked like she had moved a little since he had first found her. The little calf snuggled close to her side out of the cold wind.

It is often easy to scare a cow. Even though it appears that she cannot move, the cow is given strength by Mother Nature to evade any attempt at capture. In a cow with a uterine prolapse, undue motion lessens her chance of survival, because motion can disturb ruptured vessels and add to trauma. Jim pointed the lights of his pickup on the cow while I sneaked out of the dark and caught her around the horns. The rope hitting her head brought her to her feet, and away she took me. Jim saved the day when he caught up with me; his additional 250 pounds pulled her to an abrupt halt. I backed my car around and we anchored her to the trailer hitch. She got on the fight real quick and speared a taillight out with her horn. I heeled her to prevent further damage to her or to the car, and we stretched her out to the front bumper of Jim's pickup. We were ready to go to work.

In order to replace a uterus, a spinal anesthetic has to be administered. This stops all pain and any continued labor as the uterus is manipulated. After anesthetic, the cow is rolled up on her brisket. The hanging uterus is cleansed and washed with disinfectant, and the fetal membranes are removed if possible. The whole organ is then packed back inside.

On that night, I had Jim stand astraddle of the cow, holding her in the brisket position with her tail in one hand and his flashlight in the other. A prolapsed uterus is not easy to replace, and I needed more than the two hands the good Lord had given me. As I put pressure on one area, another would bulge out. It was a slow process. I was thankful for the hot water we used as the cold wind stung my hands. After repeated efforts the uterus finally disappeared into its proper place. I straightened it out and packed it with antibiotic powder. Sutures were taken to prevent reoccurrence of the condition. I gave her the usual dose of penicillin and started cleaning up after such an ordeal.

While I was putting my instruments away, Jim found the calf, which had disappeared as we roped his mother. He had cuddled up under a clump of brush not thirty feet from where we had been working on the cow. Jim threw out half a bale of hay and a bale of straw for the pair. I untied the cow. As she staggered to her feet, she took one good pass at me with her pointed horns. After that she moved over to where her calf was lying, gave him a nuzzle, and trotted off into the darkness with the calf wobbling behind. I had done my part, and now I only hoped Mother Nature would give me a little help with the cow's recovery and the calf's new life. I said goodnight to Jim and headed for home with a roar and one taillight hanging out of its socket in the night.

I wondered what my insurance man would say when I told

him about the car the next morning. If insurance wouldn't pay for everything, financially speaking I would have been ahead if I had stayed home and retired to my bed. In terms of accomplishment, though, the money didn't matter that much. The sight of that cow trotting off with her calf had been reward enough.

THE JARINA BROTHERS

THE JARINA BROTHERS LIVED IN THE FOOTHILLS UNDER THE shadow of the great Rocky Mountains. They weren't exactly hermits, but their living was simple. Power lines went all the way to their front yard, but the brothers never bothered to connect them. They very seldom washed their dishes; mostly they just licked them clean and turned them over. Their beds were rarely made, and their floors certainly weren't worn out from sweeping. Consequently, they very seldom had any company.

As the years went by, even the Jarina ranch buildings and corrals began to disintegrate. The men raised cattle in a lackadaisical manner, and once in a while they would call on me to doctor an animal that was usually about to die. I saved a few and lost a few. They never failed to inform me of my losses.

One particular call from the Jarinas was an obstetric case that should have been taken care of about two days previously. As a

THE CROSS THREE RANCH ON THE TWO MEDICINE RIVER.

last hope, the brothers had driven twenty-one miles into town to give the old vet a ring. Since the beginning days of my practice, I had a standing offer: I would doctor a cow in exchange for half of it. In later years, I had few clients who made such a gamble. Mike Jarina, the brother who owned the cow in this case, sensing the severity of her condition, asked me if I would take one-half for my fee. He figured she was very likely going to die.

"I certainly will," I said and went about my business of performing a caesarean section.

About halfway through the operation—which wasn't going too well due to the emphysematous condition of the fetus—I looked up and saw a quizzical look on old Mike's face. "Don't faint," I told him, "I might need your help in case I run into more trouble."

"No," he said, "I was just wondering what healthy cows were worth on the market now."

"You mean a cow like this, if she lives?" I asked.

"Yes," he said. I told him I thought she might bring about $180 if she were in good shape.

Mike came right out with it, then, as he looked down at the poor old cow that I admit was in pretty sad shape at the moment. "Will you give me $90 for my half right now?" he asked.

That set me back a minute, but since I had already gambled a little, gambling some more couldn't hurt. I took the deal.

Well, I finished the operation, cleaned my instruments, and wrote Mike a check for $90. That was the first time I ever paid a client to allow me to drive seventy-five miles and do a c-section on a dying patient. As I drove away down the road, I wondered what old Mike was thinking after I left. I imagined he figured he had really put one over on me. I wasn't so sure he hadn't.

About two months later, I ran into Mike and his brother, John, and I'll be damned if they didn't ask me when I was coming up to get my cow. "Besides that," they said, "we have some others we would like to sell you." They must have figured I was a pretty easy mark.

Six Shooter Sam

IT WAS A VERY WINDY AFTERNOON. A SUNDAY AFTERNOON, to be exact, and I had been called by the manager of a large ranch to ascertain the cause of death of several calves that had just been weaned.

In my part of the country, wind comes when air falls off the mountains, its velocity increasing enough to reach one hundred miles per hour or more. Small lakes develop whitecaps and water streamers that irrigate their lee sides to quite a distance. Streams are practically whipped dry, and that may be the reason they sometimes go underground . . . to protect themselves. As one of my old rancher friends says, "It's the kind of a day you have to put a gunny sack under the horse's tail to keep the wind from blowing the bit out of his mouth."

On such windy days, it is impossible to hear. I usually pull my ear flaps down, and even then the whistling and popping of the gusts shuts off the auditory complex. Wind also makes people grumpy. More suicides are committed on windy days than on still, beautiful days when the song of a meadowlark can be heard for nearly a mile.

I could go on and on with windy tales about our great Rocky Mountain front, but I'll get back to my story. After sixty miles traveling crossways to the wind, I arrived at the pasture where I was supposed to meet McGillis, the ranch manager. No one was around, so I bounced around the badger holes and finally located three dead calves. I parked my car in such a way that it would protect me from the wind as much as possible, and went to work performing an autopsy. I was engrossed in my job, bending down, examining all tissues closely, setting aside an occasional sample to be biopsied or cultured. The sounds of the wind precluded any extraneous noises or sounds, and I was quite interested in my extensive findings. Nothing bothered me until I felt a pressure on the back of my head and heard a voice that roared over the wind say, "Caught you red-handed this time. Throw down that knife and get your hands in the air."

I knew it wasn't April Fool's Day, and I was so surprised that I immediately complied. I stood up, turned around, and looked straight into the muzzle of a .45 revolver. The hole on its end looked a lot bigger than .45 of an inch when it was one foot away from my eyeball.

In our country, there had been reported a goodly number of cattle rustlings and mutilations. The State Livestock Commission had recently underwritten a campaign to alert all ranchers and law departments to be on the lookout for such offenses. An eager young deputy figured he had hit the jackpot when he found me doing a necropsy on a dead beef.

It took a great deal of explaining that I was only doing my job, and I could see he was still skeptical after a few minutes of questioning. Rather than being on the receptive end of a trigger-happy undersheriff, I started packing up to accompany him to the county courthouse, another forty miles out of my way, when McGillis made a timely appearance and explained that all was on the up and up.

I asked the deputy if I could donate a steak from a freshly butchered animal that had recently succumbed to the ravages of mucopurulent pneumonitis. He declined, but I still felt like forcefeeding him when I remembered that cannon staring me in the face, the muzzle of his .45.

PREPARING ELK AFTER A HUNTING TRIP.

MILK FEVER

IN COWS, MILK FEVER IS QUITE COMMON. IT IS A condition that usually occurs at calving time. The production of milk takes a great deal of calcium, and quite frequently so much calcium is removed from the bloodstream that an animal can become comatose. The common name given to the condition is a misnomer, since there is no fever involved. In fact, an affected animal's temperature usually drops below normal. All body functions slow down to the point where only faint signs of life can be detected, and the symptoms can strike rapidly.

One story I can tell relating to milk fever involved old Tronson, a typical homesteader of my part of the country. Tron had taken up his 160 acres and eventually increased it to 320. He and his wife had raised a family of pretty girls. Being a scarce commodity, the young ladies had been snatched up quickly by more prosperous farmers in the area, leaving Tronson and his wife alone, eking a living out of what is considered a small parcel of land in our vast Montana country. Mrs. Tronson always had a big garden, and Mr. Tronson milked three or four cows to provide a cream check that paid for needed groceries.

Tronson's cow, Old Boss, had blossomed forth with a big healthy calf one day, and at six the next evening, when Tron went to chase the cows in for milking, she was staggering a little. By the time he milked the other cows, the new mother was restless and moving uncomfortably, continually shifting her weight from one hind hoof to the other as if her udder was hurting. Tron sat down to milk her and, all of a sudden, she fell over on him, pinning him beneath the great mass of her body.

He was unable to extricate himself. When he didn't come in for supper at the usual time, his wife stuck her head out the door and gave the "Yoo-hoo" supper call. She heard his call for help in reply, and found him in the predicament, from which she was able to extract him. After determining that he had no serious ailments, they began to ponder the course to take in regard to Old Boss.

Tron had seen milk fever a few times before in his life, but had never experienced it in one of his own animals, especially his favorite milk cow. In one case he had seen, the owner had taken a tire pump and by some method had pumped the udder plumb full of air. The cow recovered after a few hours, but died a few days later from a gangrenous udder. In another case, nothing had been done, and that cow lay in a coma for three days before finally passing on to greener pasture.

Somewhere Tronson had heard there was a new vet in the country, so he started the old pickup and drove twenty miles to his son-in-law's place to get him to locate the fellow. His son-in-law had a phone installed recently, so finding the vet shouldn't take too long, he thought.

It was about ten o'clock at night when my phone rang. "Here we go again," I thought. Many a time, when someone has a sick animal, they look at it all day long, maybe give it some home remedy treatment, and then worry about it all evening. Just before retiring, they decide to take one last look at the critter to see how she is doing. If Mother Nature or the self-administered treatment haven't done a proper job, they call the veterinarian, as a last resort. This must ease the worrier's mind, because he has done everything possible. The cases aren't usually serious.

This one was. Old Tron really needed help; to him, it was a catastrophe. There was an urgent pleading in his voice that could be detected even over the static and buzzing of a rural telephone. His concern for his favorite milk cow was genuine. There was a strong emotional factor between the owner and the animal.

It was about thirty-five or forty miles to the old Tronson homestead. Tron had given me proper directions, and after a right turn at the schoolhouse, a left turn at the "Y," another right three miles down the road to the second farm on the left, I arrived on the scene.

Tron was waiting impatiently, waving a flashlight to beckon me to the barn. He reminded me of a dog joyously greeting his master. He would run to me, then back to the old cow, trying to get me to hurry a little faster. He did this two or three times while

I was getting an intravenous solution hooked up with tubes and needles for the administration. All the time, he felt she was dying, but he kept asking me if I thought I could save her.

The cow was in a deep coma. Her eyes were glassy, and she wouldn't even exhibit a palpebral reflex. Her ears were cold, and even though a cow is not supposed to sweat, there were beads of water on every hair. Her blood pressure and heartbeat were barely perceptible; her breathing, though even, was very weak. To old Tron and possibly anyone else observing her, she was on her last leg as an earthly creature.

Somehow, I was lucky, and the needle slipped into the jugular vein on the first attempt. I hooked up the intravenous tube, and calcium solution began to trickle into her bloodstream. After about one hundred cubic centimeters of solution had gone in, an eyelid moved. Another hundred ccs caused the muscles over her entire body to start twitching and trembling. Her heartbeat quickened and was even audible as the third hundred ccs dripped in. At that point, I slowed down the rate of administration by lowering the height of the bottle, since too much calcium reaching the heart muscles will cause them to freeze and stop the heart from beating.

It takes about ten to fifteen minutes to administer the entire five-hundred-cc dose. I usually give the owner the job of holding the bottle. If you have ever tried to hold your arm straight out for five minutes, you know why. It is during dosing time that I come to learn of family histories, politics, weather, and the price of rice in China.

As the last of the solution went into Old Boss's vein, the cow began to struggle slightly, attempting to raise her head. When the last of the solution disappeared down the I.V. tube, the cow gave a big sigh, rolled up on her brisket, and started looking around. I had Tron pull her calf out of the stall; at the sight of him, she gave a motherly bellow and was up on her feet extending the tender loving care of a mother toward its offspring.

No cure in bovine medicine is more spectacular than the cure of milk fever. I felt that it was probably the major contributing factor in the advancement of veterinary medicine in large animals. When word got around that a veterinarian could bring a cow that was practically dead back to normal in a few minutes, his fame spread. The prairie telegraph is the best advertisement there is.

I left the Tronson place with two weeks' supply of eggs, cream, and the most delicious cinnamon rolls I had ever tasted. I also carried with me a feeling of profound satisfaction at having contributed a little part to the good of the world. And old Tron did his part for advertising. Every rancher in his area seemed to think I could repeat the miracle and cure every milk-fevered cow.

FIRE ENGINE PRACTICE

I CAN'T IMAGINE THE PRACTICE OF VETERINARY MEDICINE ever being dull. When I awoke to my job every morning, I never knew when and where I would end up before the day was over. In my practice, we had two-way radios installed in the cars in order to communicate better what was happening during the day. I can recall calling in to the base station from sixty to eighty miles away, or hearing the words "KOL 652. This is the base. Over." Over the years, the radio saved us countless miles in the huge country we covered. But oftentimes it meant that when we started out in the morning, we could be kept out all day on emergency calls. This happened especially during the spring months of March and April when dystocias, prolapses, milk fevers, and many other conditions made for sick neonatal calves.

One day that sticks in my mind was a bad, stormy one. I had been very busy, rushing here, there, and everywhere, finally getting home around 10 P.M. after having put in my first sixteen hours. I hit the bed and fell asleep . . . but not for long. A man called to inform me that his car had stalled in the storm, and he had called his wife to inform her of the misfortune. He told me that their milk cow had just calved and had developed milk fever. It needed immediate attention.

I struggled out of my nice, warm bed and picked him up at the local tavern from which he had called. By this time it was snowing and blowing very hard. With the experience of traveling in bad weather over bad roads for years, we set out for Shelby, Montana, a distance of twenty-five miles. I could tell before we had gone very far that the caller had been drinking considerably. Maybe he had thrown down two or three boilermakers (each a double shot of whiskey, backed by a beer chaser). That drink mixture seemingly puts immediate warmth in the body, but also rattles the brain. Anyway, he seemed to handle his booze quite well, and we had a humorous and pleasant visit while penetrating the constant barrage of snowflakes piercing the headlights and falling against the windshield. He even asked about the price I charged for the trip. "One dollar a mile plus time and medicine for the call," I replied. I thought I detected a sigh of relief then, as I herded the car between two ditches and we neared our destination.

We finally reached the town of Shelby, and my rider asked if we could stop at the Sports Club, a popular tavern in the downtown district. This I did. Once there, he jumped out, saying he would be right back. He returned in a couple of minutes and threw a twenty-dollar bill and a five-dollar bill in my lap.

He took his leave, then, stating, "I really don't have a cow. But when I got stranded in Conrad, the taxi service told me it would cost fifty bucks for a ride on a night like this." With that statement and some final words about how he knew I would do it a lot cheaper, he disappeared into the darkness of the night.

NORDEN AND THE SKUNKS

CALVING SEASON WAS NEARLY OVER, AND MY GOOD friend, Norden, the M.D., had come into possession of a complete batch of skunks, four to be exact. He called me up after supper one nice spring evening and asked if I would help de-scent them. Hell, there was nothing to it, he said. Just carve out their anal glands. Besides, little skunks like that didn't stink, anyway. He had had them around the house for four days already, and they didn't smell at all. They sure would make nice pets, besides being elegant conversation subjects.

I think my instructors had spent all of ten minutes in school discussing these exotic pets. "Keep them out of the office," was their first warning. Second was, "Little skunks do have the ability to stink," and third was, "Most of you will never be bothered with a skunk practice, so we won't spend much time on it." As a result, I knew very little, if anything, about skunks. So I was happy to oblige Norden, in exchange for his help when I was afflicted with brucellosis.

Norden arrived with his box containing the cute little things, sporting a new tie his daughters had just given him for his birthday. He was dressed in his usual suit, having just made the rounds at the hospital on his way out to see me. I tried to convince him that we should use some sort of anesthesia so the creatures wouldn't stink up the place. No, he said, he had heard that they were so small that Nembutal would kill them.

I wasn't convinced at all,

GROUSE HUNTING WITH NORDEN (DR. PORTER CANNON).

48

but Nembutal was the method they had recommended in school. To be safe, we took some phenobarbital instead, diluted it ten to one, and proceeded to give each skunk a peritonal injection. Sure enough, the cute little things slowly began to wobble and finally attained complete anesthesia.

Giving into the superiority of an M.D., I told Norden he was to do the surgery on the first one; I was to be the holder. I gingerly presented the working end of one skunk to him. He had his scalpel and forceps ready as I pressed lightly on the abdomen in order to protrude the external orifice of the anal sacs. He applied the forceps to the nipple, and with dexterity began extracting and peeling out the sac.

"This is simple," he informed me as he went about his work with all the skill of an experienced surgeon. This was repeated on the second sac and we had one de-scented skunk. All it had to do now was to recover from anesthesia.

I was awed by his success and we changed sides for me to work on the second one. I wasn't at all impressed at standing in the direct line of the working end of a skunk, but, with his expertise and guidance, first one sac and then the other was removed. I was beginning to enjoy this new experience—so far so good! The second skunk was put in the box with the first one.

It was Norden's turn again. I thought I perceived a slight movement in the third skunk as I picked him up, and mentioned this to the good doctor, but he paid it no mind and went right to work. With each movement of the scalpel I could feel the muscles tense in the tiny animal. The first gland was removed with no trouble. About halfway through the removal of the second sac, our little skunk was beginning to squirm uncomfortably. The orifice and those sacs are very fragile, and it doesn't take much pressure to tear them off. This happened. All at once, the forceps slipped off and a golden stream of the most odoriferous liquid was streaming down Norden's brand new tie. How it missed his chin I'll never know, but that ended his term of surgery.

"What the hell do I do now?" he demanded.

I told him my mother burned my clothes when as a youngster I was sprayed after I had tried to kill a trapped skunk with a club. I also suggested ammonia and a tomato-juice bath. That ended the surgical episode for Norden, except that his clients noticed he had a different air about him for a few days. Norden never helped me de-scent any more skunks.

Back at the operation, the smell attracted all the youngsters in the vicinity to the scene. All the little skunks were recovering from the anesthesia, so I dropped the last two in a gallon jar with some cotton soaked in ether and finished the job with a crowd of young spectators surrounding me. By that time I was permeated with the odor, but getting used to it. I sent Norden his two pets the next day, but I don't think his wife let him keep them around the house for a while. After about a week the smell dissipated around the office, and clients began to come and see me again.

It didn't take the kids long to spread the word around town. Our college dean said that as a veterinarian we would be "marked men," but little did I know then that I would be marked the hard way.

BRAIN SURGERY

EVERY SPRING, AS THE GRASS STARTS TO SPROUT AND THE immense grasslands take on a green hue, cows and their new calves get restless and start roaming the fence lines in search of greener pastures. Before they can be turned out or trailed to the summer ranges, a few operations have to be performed that identify, protect, and start them on the proper trail as a renewable resource in the world food chain. Each ranch accomplishes these operations in its own way, but most ranches share some common methods. They also have social facets, and turn the work into celebrations that have become fundamental and glorious parts of the cattle industry.

The old timers had a way of putting this levity into words. "A critter had to get his ole hide sizzled and his little ears tickled," they said, referring to branding and ear marking of more modern times. As time progressed, new and different methods of keeping herd health have been adopted; the modern day calf ends up lopsided from ear tags, inoculations, growth stimulants, and the final act of castration, or "brain surgery." A few operators stick to

A TYPICAL BRANDING OPERATION.

the old chuckwagons and range roundups in the spring, but even these traditionalists have lost the true romance of the cattle industry with the addition of 4x4 pickup trucks, helicopters, spectators, and microwave ovens.

Modern branding bees sometimes remind me of "beer busts" or "keggers." Beer and other potent drinks have become as commonplace as the old-fashioned pot of beans. In some instances, competition in alcohol consumption rivals that of the roper's or heeler's ability to "double hock" calves without a miss. I've been in on a few brandings where inebriation seems to be the mode of all participants. By the time cocktail hour rolls around at some of the more sophisticated bees, the people need more attitude ajustment than the brain surgeon inflicts on bull calves.

You ask why I call the man who does this necessary operation a brain surgeon? Well, the removal of gonads permanently alters the minds of male calves. It changes their minds from ass to grass!

SIDELINES: THE RODEO

RODEO ON THE OPEN RANGE.

AFTER A STRENUOUS AND BUSY SPRING, MY FRIEND Roger, who was also a veterinary student, came to stay with me. His primary concern was learning about the practice of veterinary medicine. During the summer, business was not as booming and the number of "fire engine" emergency calls began to diminish, leaving us more time to cultivate small animal practice. We clipped dogs, spayed cats, de-scented more skunks, vaccinated horses, and did all the other various and sundry things that go with a mixed veterinary practice.

There was also more time for play. Roger and I spent a number of evenings enjoying the companionship and stories of Frank at the local bar. We also consumed enormous quantities of beer. Roger didn't like to drink just one or two beers; he had to have a whole barrel of it. There seemed to be no end to his capacity of consumption. He could put the liquor away all night long with no visible change in him, except for more frequent calls to the bathroom.

Since I was supplying him with board and room, and since the board consisted of supplying the beer, I could envision a dwindling economic picture. "Roger," I said, "let's try something new. Let's get us a horse and try roping a few calves." This must have touched a chord of desire in his heart, and he was all for it. He promised to cut down on beer consumption if we could practice roping calves every evening. I think he had visions of

53

becoming a champion rodeo hand.

I went down to my brother's auction sale barn and came back the new owner of a guaranteed rope horse, four hundred bucks worth of animal. Little did I know that we also needed an arena, roping calves, ropes, rope cans, skid boots, tie downs, breast collars, and, last but not least, a trailer to haul old Chubby, the rope horse, around. On top of that were spurs, pigging strings, and a roping bit. I already had a saddle. We also needed a bigger car to pull the trailer, since a good headwind would halt progress completely in my sixty-five horsepower model.

By the time we were outfitted, instead of having visions of being a champion calf roper, I had visions of being a bankrupt pauper. Where in hell did that wild hair come from anyway? In spite of all the pecuniary adjustments, we managed to complete the menagerie and faithfully spent many evenings attempting to rope calves. If we were lucky, we would catch maybe half of the calves we tried to rope. We came up with many empty loops, and once in a while I thought I could discern a note of discord in poor old Chubby. "If they're going to spend all their time missing, why should I try so hard?" he must have thought.

It's no fun roping by yourselves all the time, so Roger and I decided after a few weeks that we had better try our luck at a rodeo. We heard of a friendly roping contest at a nearby town and decided to enter.

We arose early that Sunday, put on our finest duds, gathered our gear, and loaded up old Chubby. Away we went. It was only forty miles to the rodeo, with no steep hills, so we made it with time to spare. Our under-powered jitney and our double-eagle onionskin tires held up in good shape.

Since it was to be a friendly rodeo, we went to look up the secretary to pay our entry fees. "Twenty-five bucks apiece, plus fifteen for dues," she announced as she scanned the entry sheets. Right then and there the roping ceased to be just friendly. The eighty dollars we had to come up with taxed my financial statement to the utmost. Unless we got some return on our investment, there would be little beer and less food in the weeks ahead. I had visions of good old Frank being our benefactor for the next few days.

We managed to look at a few horses while we were waiting for the rodeo to begin. We met many people and lined up a few calls for the days ahead. We also kept our eyes open for a caddy; all the cowboys seemed to have a female friend to look after their equipment and to exercise their horse while they threw ropes at hay bales, rope cans, or weeds. We didn't want to be different, so we threw ropes with them. Roger even found a friend to ride Chubby around the arena, and we truly felt we were part of the whole scene. It was exhilarating, to say the least.

At last the moment arrived. Roger was up first and he looked like a regular professional as he backed Chubby into the box for his debut into the competitive rodeo world. As he nodded his head for the calf to be turned loose, all signs of professionalism disappeared. During practice we had never bothered to string a barrier in front of the horse to prevent premature starting. Chubby must have thought the string was a hurdle: with a great leap, he jumped it on his way out. I could see the entire Rocky Mountain range between Roger and the saddle as Chubby cleared the barrier without even touching it. There was a conglomeration of ropes, arms, hat, and dust as the calf, the horse, and Roger went full-speed down the arena.

Chubby, after his jump, finally caught up with the calf. Being tired, he then stopped, just as Roger threw a desperate loop. This must have caught Roger off-balance. Instead of making a nice clean get-off, he ended up rolling like a ball on the ground. The calf was caught, and Roger finally collected himself and started to tie the calf down. In the commotion, the pigging string dropped from his mouth, and Roger, in disgust, finally jerked the loop off the calf's head and turned him loose. The crowd roared with laughter as he rode humbly back through the arena. "That's a quick way to blow twenty-five bucks," he informed me. I asked if he had hurt anything, and he replied, "Nothing but my pride." A couple of beers repaired his pride, and it was his turn to watch.

Before my turn came, we gave Chubby a quick education on

running through a barrier string. My attempt was more successful, and at the close of the events, I ended up in the money—fourth place. My winnings totaled up to $32.50. We were only about fifty bucks in the hole after our first big day at the rodeo.

No rodeo is complete without some of the social life that goes with it. Roger collected his caddy and with her sympathy and a few extra bottles of beer we started for home. To get there, it so happened that we had to pass through one little town. We stopped, and immediately Roger began to drown his sorrows. His caddy friend decided it was probably better to go home with her parents, or maybe they decided it, and Roger and I began to make the rounds at the three bars where festivities were picking up as the evening progressed. There were jukeboxes blaring and people bellied up to the bar everywhere. Stories were retold. Drinks were plentiful.

We still had quite a distance to go, so I tried to convince Roger we should head for home. While I visited with some newly made friends, Roger took off. He headed for the car and trailer and gave good old Chubby a few reassuring pats. One thing led to another as he took him from the trailer to rest his weary bones. Being a little on the tipsy side and seeing poor old Chubby standing there cold sober brought another thought into his head. Old Chubby needed a beer like the rest of us. Into the bar they went, Chubby acting as if he were an everyday customer, taking a few licks of spilled beer with his tongue.

News of this incident soon reached me, and I arrived on the scene about the same time a deputy sheriff did. He quickly informed Roger that it was contrary to a city ordinance for horses to be drinking with their friends in a bar.

"Chubby can't read," Roger replied. "Besides, this is the only waterhole around this joint, and he was just as thirsty as me. You can't put a horse in jail."

"No, but I can sure put you there," the deputy replied. "You can take your horse out and come with me."

I tried to talk the lawman out of putting an innocent, impoverished college student into the bastille. It didn't help. "If you want your friend, you come down and give us ten bucks. Then we'll give him back to you," he said.

I put Chubby back into the trailer and walked into the jail as the heavy iron door closed behind Roger. Further pleading Roger's cause was to no avail. It took my last dollar to purchase his freedom. We headed for home after our first day at the rodeo, broke, half drunk, and a little more experienced in the ways of the world.

BAD BRAHMA BULL

VETERINARIANS OFTEN FIND THEMSELVES IN PRECARIOUS situations. One day at the local "Whoop-Up" rodeo, a bucking bull would not go into the catch pen after he had been bucked out. The pick-up men roped him two times and finally dragged him into the catch pen. But before he could be run through the chute to where his bull comrades were, the gate leading into the catch pen was opened to admit another bull, and Mr. Brahma, with two ropes dragging, escaped into the general arena. Again, he refused to go into the catch pen, and in despair took a running jump and cleared the arena fence like a trained jumping horse. Several team ropers took after him, adding two more ropes to his head before he escaped through a couple of barbed wire fences. When last seen, he was heading for the Dry Fork breaks and freedom.

The stock contractor left town minus one good brahma bucking bull, after the local banker . . . who fancied himself a cowboy . . . told the contractor he would scour the country and be responsible for corralling the stray bull as soon as possible. He found the bull, alright, running with a bunch of registered Hereford cows and adding his exotic genes to the well-bred herd. The owner of the Herefords said he didn't need any of this genetic engineering, and requested the bull be removed from the premises. The entire herd was corralled, and the brahma was cut out in a separate pen. By this time, he had several practice sessions in the fence-jumping business, so it wasn't long before he was seen heading for the Dry Fork badlands and another spell of freedom. He didn't seem to mind all the ropes dragging behind.

I've always accused bankers of having I.Q.s lower than a snake's belly in a wagon track. They like to lend money when cattle are high and sell out when they are low. They are very consistent in this pattern, and I often have wondered how most of them ever got through the seventh grade. It must be that if they did things right, loans would get paid . . . so no one would need to borrow more money. This particular banker wasn't much better than his colleagues; as a cowboy he was even worse.

First, he rented an airplane and found the bull again. He and a few sidewalk cowboys, the entire search-and-rescue team, and even the sheriff's posse tried for the next two weeks to capture the brahma without success. Finally, he called me to see if I had a tranquilizer gun he could borrow. I refused him the loan of the gun for several reasons, the main one being that a tranquilizer gun in the hands of an inexperienced person is a dangerous weapon. I've seen everything from grizzly bears to numerous game animals killed by improper usage. I did not want to be responsible for the demise of a good bucking brahma bull owned by my rodeo stock contractor and old friend Horace. So the banker asked if I would assist him in capturing the brahma bull. I reluctantly said yes, on the condition that he call off the army of would-be rescuers and let me know the next time the bull was spotted. This he agreed to do.

About two days later, I received a call informing me that the bull was seen in a wheat field grazing the newly sprouted crop. I jumped my trusty old calf-roping horse in the trailer and headed for the country. Sure enough, the old brahma was grazing contentedly in the middle of the field. I found the longest lariat that I owned and headed out to meet him. I circled him a couple of times and finally got him started in the right direction. There was a good set of corrals six feet high about two miles away. Everything went fine until the old boy got a little tired; all he would do then was turn, face me, and shake his horns in a menacing way.

I finally decided that if I wanted to bring the bull in, it would have to be on the end of a rope. I must have been lucky that day, because my loop settled over Mr. Brahma's horns on the first try. I jerked up the slack and took a couple of dallies as he made a run for me. My old rope horse, Pokey by name, came to life and took off as I threw a couple of dallies. The old bull loped behind, and I headed for the corral. Once or twice he stopped, and I gave him a good jerk or two while avoiding his charges.

I don't know whether or not all those ropes dragging off the bull had made his head sore and tender but it wasn't long before he acted like he had been halter broke. He was soon following behind me like a gentle old milk cow. I think he took about two more charges at the old horse, then settled down to a steady gait right into the set of corrals.

About the time the banker drove up, we closed and latched the gate behind old Brahma. He had seven ropes on him at the time. With a few bull-fighting maneuvers, I trapped him in a smaller pen leading up a runway into the loading chute. Up he came, and I trapped him there, too, with a big stout post so he couldn't escape.

The old bad brahma must have figured he was ready for another great rodeo performance. He stood there while I removed my rope and all the others. I sent the banker for a truck with a good stout rack, coiled up all the ropes, threw them in the trailer, loaded "Ole Pokey," and headed back to the vet hospital.

The experience of the chase was worth it. I never had to buy another nylon rope for about five years. A good way to break in a rope is to drag it around for a week or two, and old Brahma had done an excellent job. Besides that, my banker became more friendly. When I borrowed money after that he never tried to tell me how to spend it!

MAD BULL

SOME ANIMALS SENSE THAT A VETERINARIAN IS HELPING them; others take the opposite view. Time and time again, when I've pregnancy-tested a cow, she has jumped out of the squeeze chute, gone about ten feet, then turned around to look back at me as if to say, "Now, why did you do that to me?" after I've run my arm up her rectum about two feet to palpate her uterus. Other cows will jump out, displaying a burst of speed as if they're running to escape the death sentence . . . which they have, if they are not pregnant. Rarely, cows will turn around and clear onlookers and chute help out of the way in the bellicose manner of a famous fighting bull.

After years of experience, I can usually determine the disposition of an animal when I go to work on it. The usual quip about an angry animal is that he or she displays qualities of a female disposition, hot and cold. There is always the exception to the rule, though, and we run across a male animal that, depending on the breed or the environment, doesn't appreciate restraints or various treatments.

One day I was called to treat a bull for a disease we call lump jaw. There was no one home at the ranch when I arrived, so I went out to the corral and found the bull placidly chewing his cud, oblivious to any condition he might have. He was in an old round corral with a big post in the middle that had served many years as the main pen for forefooting horses and castration of stallions.

I laid a "hoolihan loop" over the bull's horns. The bull didn't mind this too much. I then proceeded to heel him and snub him to the stoutest post I could find on the outside fence. This perturbed him a little, but he didn't show any signs of complete rage. I could not throw him or tail him down by myself, so I put another hitch on him that has always worked for me. This hitch consists of a bowline noose around the neck followed by two half-hitches, one around the rib cage and another around the flanks. When I pull this tight, the bovine usually collapses and remains down while the hitch remains taut.

Restraint is ninety percent of veterinary medicine, so before any further procedure, I put on a pair of nose tongs and tightened the line as much as possible. Then I went to work. First I gave him an intravenous injection of sodium iodide; next I proceeded to lance and pack the huge abscess that caused the lump on his jaw. The bull took exception to this procedure, and I was wishing that a good squeeze chute was available to facilitate my job.

I finished my course of treatment and began to remove all the bull's restraints. I got them all off and removed from the corral, with the exception of my lariat that I left next to the central snubbing post. I had no more picked it up when, out of the corner of my eye, I saw a ton of mad bull hurtling himself toward me in an unfriendly fashion. I jumped for the protection of the central post at the same time his massive head collided with the opposite side. There we were, eyeball to eyeball: I can't tell you whose eyes were bigger, his or mine. All I know is they were very close together, with only the protection of a post between us.

The bull would not give up, and continued to circle and hit the post, his pointed horns protruding on either side of the post as I dodged and used all the evasive tactics I knew. He could circle that post nearly as fast as I could, and his ire seemed to increase with the passage of time. Usually an animal will take one or two charges, then back off and look for an open gate or an escape route. This was not the mad bull's style. He stood

OPENING THE DROP FENCE GATE ON THE TRAIL TO THE MOUNTAIN PASTURE.

there with his eyes intent on reaching my anatomy for what seemed nearly an eternity.

While fighting the bull, I had an old story pop into my mind. The story went something like this: a veterinarian had gone out to treat a bull similar to the one I had just treated, except it was of a dairy breed. Dairy bulls are usually more unpredictable than beef bulls. There are many instances where dairy bulls have maimed or killed people. In that particular case, the bull had charged the veterinarian, run a horn through his chest, and pinned him to a board fence. The bull had been unable to extricate himself from the knothole that his horn penetrated, and there he stood with the vet hanging from the horn. About thirty minutes later, the farmer came home, cut off the bull's horn, and removed the doctor to the hospital. The vet survived, and when people asked if it hurt much when he was hanging there, his answer was, "Only when I laughed!"

For about twenty minutes, I hung, too, in my own predicament. Then my adversary turned tail, and I made a mad dash for the rail fence, clearing it with an acrobatic move that probably could be in the *Guinness Book of World Records*. I packed my ropes and instruments into the car. As I went on my way, thankful that I was not in a bad condition, I could laugh without it hurting at all.

FOURTH OF JULY

ON THE FOURTH OF JULY EACH YEAR, MONTANANS TAKE off for yearly outings to mountains, lakes, rivers, or wherever their favorite place may be. Along with them go their pets, to explore the vastness of the Big Sky Country. In the course of their explorations, the family protector often comes into contact with some of the few animals he needs protection from, and returns to the fold bedecked with a face and mouthful of porcupine quills.

No other catastrophe seems to arouse more emotional sentiments than Old Blue looking dolefully unhappy and chastised in his bewhiskered predicament. Immediate relief is sought, and Old Blue is usually attacked with a pair of pliers. He may tolerate the removal of the first quill not knowing what to expect, but the attempt to remove any more is usually met with bared fangs and a canine determination to keep the status quo.

Since man's best friend has turned against him, outside help in the form of human friends is obtained. They usually offer only the "good" advice to cut off the quills so they will come out easier. Having explored all avenues of pulling quills out of a dog's mouth and getting no satisfactory results, somebody recalls that the new veterinarian might be able to help. In the meantime, Old Blue sits around wondering about some porcupine walking around in the woods half-naked.

My first call on July 4 came at six o'clock in the morning. The Anderson family had arrived home at midnight. With Blue still resisting all attempts to have any more quills removed, they wondered if I would come down to the office and give them a hand. When I arrived, the entire family, including Blue, was waiting at the door. After spending a night with a face and mouth full of bristling quills, Blue was wondering what other calamity might befall him. The Andersons were apologetic for bothering me at this hour, especially on a holiday. They had taken off for the mountains after work the day before and were lamenting over the fact that Blue's first encounter with porcupine had ruined their planned holiday. "We called early so we would catch you before you left for someplace," they asserted.

Blue was placed on the table and in about thirty seconds was asleep from an intravenous anesthetic. A thorough examination revealed quills dispersed throughout the tongue, oral cavity, nose, lips, and face. The entire family wondered when I was going to start cutting them off so they would pull out easier. I grabbed a hemostat and began the slow process of pulling quills. The little Anderson boy managed to retrieve one that had accidentally fallen on the floor and stuck it halfway into the palm of his hand. After a few tears and squeals on removal, he didn't disturb me much; he must have had more sympathy for the dog after his own accident.

Blue had done a good job on the porcupine. Instead of retreating after the first few quills penetrated his nose, he must have become angry and taken a terrible bite. If left to Mother Nature, I'm certain the porcupine would have been victorious in the end. Blue would have slowly starved to death, because there was no way he could have eaten. The pain and infection would have grown worse with each passing day. I hoped that he would appreciate my work to prevent all that, even though his mouth would be extremely tender for a few days.

The last quills were finally extracted, and Blue was carried out and laid on the car seat. He could recover from the anesthetic at home. I had a few plans of my own for the day.

I gathered my gear and was loading Chubby, my rope horse, into the trailer when a car traveling at breakneck speed turned into the dirt driveway and screeched to a halt in a cloud of dust.

"Boy, am I glad I found you," the driver said. "Duffy was nosing around some sagebrush early this morning and all of a sudden I heard him yelp. I went over to him and there was the biggest rattler you ever did see. I killed him and brought Duffy in from fifty miles out. Drove a hundred miles an hour all the way in from the lake where I was fishing. Do you think you can help him, Doc?"

Sure enough, Duffy had two fang marks along the side of his upper lip. I clipped off the hair and determined by the swelling and discoloration that it was too late to incise and apply suction. He needed antivenin, and I didn't have any. After a hasty call to the local pharmacist the antivenin was procured and administered to Duffy. I told Jim that Duffy's face would swell . . . instead of looking like a Labrador, he would look like a lion by the next morning . . . but that he would probably pull through with no aftereffects. He had probably learned his lesson and was no worse off than Old Blue, who had just been dequilled. He told me Duffy had been the porcupine route two years ago, and he had taken him one hundred miles to the nearest vet.

In parting, he asked me if I knew how porcupines had intercourse, to which I gave a negative reply. "Very carefully," he said, and drove off in a cloud of dust. He was a man in a hurry to get back to his fishing.

I loaded Chubby and drove by to wake my friend Roger to go to the rodeo. He had a hangover from the previous night's celebration and informed me he had twenty reasons for not going with me to participate in the calf roping. "Each one is a dollar," he said, so I left him to spend the day recuperating from the wages of sin.

THE OLD TIMER'S CAT

MANY PEOPLE BECOME ATTACHED TO THEIR PETS, BUT FOR some reason are reluctant to let it show. Boyd was the brand inspector at the auction yard where I had my first office. He had been a working cowboy his entire life, and we spent quite a little of our spare time together visiting. He was a good storyteller, and I liked to listen to his tales of the early days.

I also liked to visit with him because his wife was a tremendous cook. About once a week she would take me to their home and mother me like a long-lost son. She would worry that I wasn't being fed properly, and would proceed to give me a week's supply of nutrition in one meal. I had to starve myself for at least a day before accepting her invitation. The more I bragged about her cooking, the more food she would put in front of me. It was usually so good that I would have a gastric distortion after one of her meals.

They owned the prettiest green-eyed black cat I ever laid eyes on. Tom was his given name, but I don't think I ever heard Boyd call him anything but the "God-damned cat." In the gruff manner

MY GENERATION: BILL, AUDREY, DUKE, AND RIB.

67

that he spoke, you would think he hated Tom with a passion. I surmised this was untrue since there was a rapport between the cat and Boyd you couldn't help but notice. If the cat sat by the door for a minute, Boyd would ease over and open the door, by some telegraphic means knowing the cat was there. When Boyd opened the door, Tom would stalk in, arch his back, and give Boyd's boot a few tender rubs. Both Boyd and his wife saw to it that Tom never spent one hungry moment.

One day Boyd came into the office. It was during the spring rush, and I had hardly seen him for two or three weeks. After a few pleasant greetings, he told me that his missus thought the "God-damned cat" was sick. Would I come up and have a look at him?

I was happy at the thought of returning a few favors, and knew that his wife would be waiting with a gourmet spread. Besides, Boyd couldn't bring the cat in; if any of his cowboy friends saw him carting a cat around, he would be the laughingstock of the country.

Tom wasn't in very good shape when I arrived at Boyd's place. A quick examination revealed a condition quite common in old tomcats: a small kidney stone had lodged in the cat's urethra, and poor old Tom couldn't urinate. His bladder was full, and he was in extreme pain. I informed Boyd and his wife that I would have to anesthetize the cat in order to remove the stone. I took him to the office and they followed close behind.

The cat had been such a part of their lives that I knew they would be heartbroken if anything happened to him. The animal had probably replaced their children, in later years, as a member of the family. And the cat never talked back, or caused sorrowful moments, like children are wont to do. The creature had demanded the attention of both of them for years, and gave them a common ground of endearment. I knew Tom, "that God-damned cat," was one of the most important things in their lives.

They watched eagerly as I put Tom to sleep with an anesthetic. Sometimes it is difficult to remove a kidney stone, so I didn't paint any rosy picture of the outcome. For their sakes, I hoped for the best. Extrasensory perception told me what they were thinking: "Old Tom just has to pull through!"

All went well. Without any undue amount of pressure on the bladder, the stone was dislodged and the condition relieved. I gave Boyd and his wife a little lecture on the cat's new diet, and sent them home. I had hoped they might ask me about my diet, too, and have me back for a bite to eat, but I knew better. Right then, the welfare of that "God-damned cat" was the most important thing in their lives.

DISTEMPER

DISTEMPER IS THE COLLECTIVE TERM FOR A SERIES OF maladies in dogs, cats, and horses. Before the advent of modern medicine, it was Mother Nature's favorite method of controlling an animal population explosion. Periodically, the disease will hit an unprotected society of animals, spreading rapidly through its members. In its wake, it leaves many dead. In dogs, distemper may leave aftereffects that remain with them the rest of their natural lives.

I was sitting in my office one day, browsing through the numerous periodicals and brochures that somehow seem to comprise the major portion of a veterinarian's mailbag. Most of the brochures were sales-oriented epistles from drug manufacturers, expounding the virtues of each company's particular products. Many of the brochures looked the same: they each displayed a huge picture of a happy veterinarian injecting a happy dog. The dog sat happily on a table, showing no signs of fright and no indication of wanting to retaliate by giving his friendly saviour a good bite. In the picture, the dog's owner was also smiling and happy, thrilled that his or her pet had been saved. The look on his or her face indicated that they would live happily ever after.

I was in a dilemma, wanting to know which method to use to properly immunize a dog to make such healthy dogs and happy owners. I recalled spending several weeks in the "crud ward" in school, attempting to save dogs suffering from the ravages of distemper and its virus syndrome, hepatitis, or encephalitis, as the foremost authorities were beginning to call it. Vaccines for the disease were not one hundred percent effective, and the quarantined section of the school's hospital contained a few animals with vaccination histories that should have guaranteed them a disease-free life.

At the time, new distemper vaccines were hitting the market monthly. It was difficult to determine which one would give the results the advertisements so proudly proclaimed. I had already

70

tried two different brands without much success. In one case, I wondered if I hadn't actually given the dog distemper, because it showed up three weeks after vaccination with a full-blown case. There were live-virus vaccines, killed-virus vaccines, and attenuated vaccines. There were passive serum treatments and other variations and mixtures of many methods. A dog would look and feel like a pincushion if I followed all the recommended procedures. What I wanted was a simple, effective vaccine to protect all dogs from the ravages of the dreadful disease.

I was studying about these methods when a drug salesman wandered into my office. Salesmen were a rarity, because a visit to my clinic involved a two-hundred-mile trip; few would travel so far to see a neophyte veterinary practitioner. In addition, my financial statements precluded any large order.

I'll never know whether it was extrasensory perception or observation . . . the fact that I had literature scattered about on the subject of distemper . . . but the salesman raised the right topic. He had a brand-new vaccine on the market that made anything else available seem outmoded. It had been demonstrated to be the most effective, simple method ever devised, he said. In fact, it was so popular with all the other veterinarians that the supply was limited, so if I procrastinated too long it would be impossible to obtain. The man's salesmanship was superb. He touched every emotional nerve in my body and walked out leaving me with nearly a year's supply of "the best distemper vaccine on the market."

It wasn't long after that when Al walked in. He had a purebred Weimaraner bitch that had whelped and raised eight valuable offspring. Weimaraners were rare dogs, having been obtained from Germany at the close of World War II and imported to the United States to enhance the long list of canine breeds here. A prestigious clan in the canine world, Weimeraners commanded a fabulous price. As hunters, they were reckoned to be the ultimate of all bird dogs.

Al wanted all his valuable puppies immunized against distempter. I was elated: I had the new super vaccine that could really do the job! Two weeks after the puppies were weaned, he carted them down to my office, where we proceeded to vaccinate the entire litter. It looked to be a red-letter day for my practice. I had never vaccinated so many pups at one time before. Things were beginning to look up.

When the time came to settle the bill, Al informed me that he was a little short. The dogs were eating him out of house and home, and at the price he was asking, not many people had beaten a path to his door for a pup. I ventured to ask the going price, and he quoted me a whorehouse figure that made me certain I would never own one. However, since he was in a predicament and wanted to keep things clear, I agreed to be the new owner of one cute female puppy for services rendered. I was to guarantee that she would be spayed, though, so I couldn't go into competition with him in his lucrative business. That's how I came to be the proud owner of Olga, my first dog since my boyhood days on our ranch.

Olga was my constant companion. She put in many miles in the next few weeks. Her exuberance and appetite complimented one another, and only occasionally did she ever give any trouble. She would lie quietly on the seat of the car while I drove the many miles required of my expanding practice. Only the frequent passage of large amounts of gas would let me know that she was present. When we were around the office, she would move wherever I happened to go. She was beginning to retrieve an old mitten I used for training, and I was satisfied she would be the best bird dog in the world. She loved to romp and play, and showed the natural instincts of a hunter when I stopped occasionally to walk her down fence rows where pheasants had congregated.

Olga was about five months old when the first symptoms of distemper hit. She began to lose her appetite and developed diarrhea. Her eyes began to exude matter. She ran a slight temperature, and became more listless with the passage of each day. Evidently her constant exposure to the distempered dogs that I treated in the office had overcome the immunity of vaccination, or the vaccine did not cover all the strains of the distemper virus. In spite of all the precautions, my own beloved pet was the victim of a disease I had fought in years of schooling to prevent.

I gave Olga every treatment I knew. Her temperature returned to normal, and the matter around her eyes cleared up. She began to eat normally, and the diarrhea ceased. I thought that the least I could do was cure her disease if I couldn't prevent it. I had certainly cured it in the past—several of the dogs around town had been given similar treatments and had responded miraculously. Olga was doing the same, except that after two weeks the symptoms started to return.

I repeated the treatments, and Olga again returned to what I considered to be normal. She was beginning to have a few misgivings about all the attention she was getting, however. Her daily shots didn't thrill her at all, and having several pills crammed down her throat made her as shy about coming into the office as the average client's dog after a few trips to the vet. After the second series of treatments, Olga again appeared normal.

Pheasant season was approaching, and I was anxious to give Olga actual field experience. Two more weeks elapsed before I noticed anything wrong with her. She then began to develop a nervous tick in her left front leg. As she would lie, apparently asleep, in the office or car, a spasm would hit her leg about every thirty seconds. This really bothered me. I had known several dogs that developed similar aftereffects of distemper that remained with them for the rest of their lives. Olga's spasms remained constant and persistent. I gave her another series of treatments. Other than the nervous tick, she had no symptoms and seemed to be doing fine.

About three weeks later, I was working in the office one night when I heard a funny clicking noise as Olga moved around. She still had the nervous tick, but it wasn't that that caused my alarm. With each step it sounded as if a tap dancer was beginning to warm up for a performance. I gently put her up on the table, and examined her feet. The normally soft, pliable pads on every foot were as hard as rocks. Olga was afflicted with "hard pad" disease. This had been described to me in school as one of the terminal stages of distemper. It was rare for a dog to recover once it reached that stage.

I was heartbroken and angry. I was mad because the happy picture portrayed by the vaccine salesman and the drug companies wasn't true. I was heartbroken because Olga had become a part of my life, and I hurt at the thought that I would probably lose her. I had empathy for clients who had similar experiences, was humbled again, and thought to myself, "It's a hell of a note when a veterinarian can't even take care of his own dog."

Olga became progressively worse. Her pads became thicker and harder. Her nervous tick stayed the same, but her appetite diminished, and in another two weeks she developed cerebral symptoms that told me the virus had taken its toll on her entire nervous system. I made a one-hundred-mile trip to have one of my fellow practitioners euthanize poor Olga.

She was the only one of the Weimaraner litter that had any problems. I've probably been taking it out on salesmen ever since; I certainly take their pitches with a much larger grain of salt than I did with that first one who sold me the "super" vaccine.

POT LICKERS

RASTUS, THE COW DOG, WITH MY SON
BARR GUSTAFSON, D.V.M.

"POT LICKERS" IS A COLLEC-
TIVE TERM OF ENDEARMENT
for the canine species. Singular,
it was also the name of one of
my favorite cow dogs. For
word-saving purposes, "Pot
Licker" was shortened to "Lick,"
just as my own nickname was
bobbed from "Rib Tickler" to
"Rib." The name has stuck with
me my entire life.

Lick entered my life as a
little blonde furball when she
was six weeks old. A dog
trainer on his way to the great
Calgary Stampede had dropped
off her dam at the home of a
friend before crossing the international border at Sweet Grass,
Montana. My good wife gave Lick to me as a present, after paying
twenty dollars to defray the cost of her neonatal life.

This little dog was an Australian shepherd and border collie,
and exhibited signs of extreme intelligence from the very
beginning. Of course, her ancestors were all highly trained show
dogs that we see exhibited on television and in state fairs
frequently.

Lick began her training by accompanying me on all my daily
calls. Her first experiences were getting used to all the
commotion and noises around a cattle chute while working cattle.
As she became braver and older, she would occasionally trail a
cow out of the chute and attempt a nip at its heels. As she became
a little bigger, and if the animal's tail was long enough, she would
catch a free ride for a few feet. The habit remained with her for
her entire life.

Soon Lick followed me whenever I rode on a horse. Always

eager to go, she would attempt to hurry things along by an attempted nip at my horse's heels if things weren't going fast enough. This caused quite a disruptive situation one frosty morning. As I was seeing a roundup crew off, the boss's horse was making a little scene. Lick scampered around behind, unnoticed by me, and encouraged the ruckus by a goodly nip on the horse's rear fetlock. This caused a minor rodeo, and I had to confine Lick to the car at the request of the roundup foreman, who was a little shook-up.

Lick turned into one of the finest chute and cow dogs I have ever seen. She minded my commands and seemed to understand what I wanted. I could make her go to the back of the runway to bring cattle towards the squeeze chute, make her nip at the rear end instead of the front end of an individual animal, or sit attentively when she wasn't needed.

Her greatest asset, though, was her heritability. I never spayed her until extremely old age, and she produced litter after litter of puppies that I gave away. Her fame and the fame of her offspring spread, and I never had any trouble finding a home for her puppies. This also increased my small animal practice, and her progeny alone contributed to quite an increase in my income. Over the years, I finally had to build a sizeable small-and-large animal clinic that kept three veterinarians employed. This was satisfying for me since, when I first arrived in our part of Montana, it was doubted that one veterinarian could make a livelihood.

One little episode in Lick's life involved a mixed litter of puppies. I had taken her to meet a good-looking Australian shepherd with the typical glass eye. I had observed his working ability, and was very impressed. The greatest impression he made on me was his ability to jump up and sit on top of a fence post when told to do so by his owner. He was a fine cow dog and a beautiful specimen of the breed.

Anyway, the puppies came, on time after sixty-three days, and Lick was allotted the normal length of time for their rearing. I took the pick of the litter for my own use, and gave the others away. I named the dog we retained "Gus," and my oldest son Sid immediately claimed him. "Good Ole Gus," as he was finally known, turned out to be even better than his dam.

Gus lived with us his entire life, and had only one shortcoming: he didn't like cats. It was difficult for us to keep both species, given the attrition rate and lifespan of felines on the place; cats were in constant jeopardy. I even think Gus taught Lick a few tricks of the cat-catching trade. They would never attack our other pets when I was around, but I began to think that cats lived on the top of telephone poles or high in trees. In later years, when both of those dogs had expired, it only took a year for my wife Pat and I to end up with about twenty cats. I started calling our home "the cathouse!"

Lick's litter, from which we obtained Gus, marked an important point of my education in animal life. Our neighbors had a feisty little poodle that must have caught Lick behind the woodshed after her visit to the Australian shepherd. All the other puppies in that litter were cross-bred poodles, and took after that side of their family tree. It also increased the libido of our neighbor's poodle, and even though I tried, there were at least two more litters resulting from the increased hormonal desire of that little black dog.

Lick herself was no slouch in the sex game. One day, when we were spaying heifers at the Rumney Ranch up near Whiskey Gap on the Milk River, I turned around to see her all hooked up with "Old Yeller," one of the cowboy's cow dogs. Rumney assured me that he was a good cow dog, and Lick produced a huge litter of yellow shepherd puppies.

My pick of that litter was a little male puppy we named "Rastus." Rastus moved up to our ranch and spent his entire life as top dog on the Cross Three outfit. One time I took him with me to work cattle and left him home at Conrad, sixty miles from the ranch. He must not have liked city life, because two days later he disappeared. I feared we had lost him, but he turned up a few days later at our neighbor's ranch on the Two Medicine River, only five miles from the ranch. My neighbor called, and

Rastus was retrieved. He usually was kept at the ranch after that episode.

Rastus did achieve a certain amount of fame himself. We were called to test a herd of buffalo, twenty-four head to be exact, that were shipped in and given to the Blackfeet tribe. These animals were shipped under quarantine, and had to be tested for *Brucella abortus* and tuberculosis before the quarantine could be lifted. Along with these tests, it was requested that we also pregnancy-test the herd.

My eldest son, Sid, had recently received his D.V.M., and volunteered to do the job for me for the experience the chore would offer. Having been associated with different aspects of dealing with buffalo, I gladly relinquished the job to him. I felt that I had had enough experiences with artificial insemination, blood testing, dehorning, and vaccinations in my years of practice.

Buffalo can be quite stubborn and unruly at times, and they have to be handled a little differently than cattle. When one of their tails goes in the air and a big bull decides to charge, it is better not to be in the way. A charge is a good way to get them started down the alleyway toward the squeeze chute, but like the original Native Americans who decoyed huge herds of buffalo over pishkuns or buffalo jumps, those who do this had better have a clear avenue of escape.

My son took Rastus, our good chute dog, with him on that particular call, and the dog performed well. Once in a while he would stimulate an animal a little too much, and Sid's normal method of restraining the dog when he wasn't needed was to yell, "Rastus! You son-of-a-bitch, go get in the pickup!"

It so happened that there was more than one Rastus around. Practically all Blackfeet Indians are endowed with nicknames, and the chief game warden, whose given name was Lester Cobell, had a similar nickname. When the command, "Rastus . . . get in the pickup" was given, Rastus Cobell immediately complied.

My son was quite embarrassed when the chute help informed

him of the situation, and he profusely apologized to Mr. Cobell. Rastus/Lester accepted his apologies, and said he wasn't particularly fond of working buffalo anyway. He had restfully drained his thermos of coffee while watching from the safety of his pickup cab.

The moral of this story? Always check to see if anyone has the same name as your dog. Or clean up your language a little.

THE FALSE TAIL

I HAD ONE INSTRUCTOR IN SCHOOL WHO ALWAYS TOLD our veterinary class that we would be marked men. I never realized at the time how true his words would be. In more than forty years of practice, my partners and I have been known by everyone in the huge area where we practice. We are asked to donate to every charitable organization. We are asked to judge everything from dog shows to high school debates, to teach boy scouts and girl scouts animal first aid, to forecast everything from the weather to the price of livestock, to entertain at political gatherings, and even to campaign for office seekers.

Of these endeavors, the one that particularly has interested me is the judging of horses. Horse shows have been a lifelong pleasure; I never tire of viewing a beautiful horse. I have spent many years traveling throughout the United States and Canada as an approved judge for the American Quarter Horse Association.

I have never known a horse owner who didn't think that his horse was the best in existence. After a few horse shows, especially large ones where the competition is keen and the quality of the animals shown keeps improving and changing over the years, it is very difficult to win. Exhibitors resort to all sorts of amelioration in order to place and garner points for their horses. A win gives status both to the horse and breeder, and enhances the horse's value and the owner's prestige.

The desperate need to win isn't so bad out here in Montana, but I do believe in the old Blackfeet adage that carries on to this day. The Blackfeet have always contended that horses and dogs are a sign of wealth. The horse didn't arrive in this country until around 1750, but the Blackfeet are thought to have seen their first horse in 1734. They named the strange new animal the "elk dog"; this creature completely changed the Indians' lifestyle. Prior to the introduction of horses, they packed their belongings on their own backs or on travois pulled by dogs. Old tepee rings of that era indicate their lodgings were not only much smaller than today's tepees, but they were also much less mobile.

THE FALSE TAIL

A HALTER-BREAKING DEMONSTRATION FOR THE 4-H CLUB.

The horse not only changed the people's lifestyle—it was also important in the demise of the great buffalo herds. The fine horse culture continues in the Blackfeet nation today. With the advent of rodeo sports and 4-H horse shows, the Blackfeet own and show some of the finest animals in the nation. And they believe in showing their horses more in their "working clothes" rather than in the spit and polish we see in some areas of the country.

In some circles it is said that fat is a pretty color. It is difficult to judge animals displaying all stages of condition. In most cases, a judge tends to favor animals with better conditioning. The quarter horse is supposed to be shown in its natural condition, with absolutely no artificial accoutrements. The horse itself is the important thing, not its parts: the painted and shined hooves, the braided manes, the brilliantined hair coats. Silver embossed halters, bridles, and saddles are to be overlooked, along with the beautiful ladies who ride them.

The rules of judging also preclude fraternization, so the life of a proper judge is oftentimes lonely. In the show ring, the judge is the boss. The steward and his aides are the liaisons who keep the show running. The exhibitor uses all the experience and expertise to show his animal to the best advantage under the existing rules.

Rules must be made to be broken, though. Judges spend considerable time and money to learn consistent application. Seminars and continuing education are mandatory. After many years of being on the so-called "firing line," I have the utmost respect for good, honest, and thoughtful judges. Their opinion determines who wins and loses, based on what horse had the best conformation and performance. Equipment is inspected so no advantage is obtained. There are hundreds of things that come up which must be weighed to render fair decisions.

One day, while I was inspecting a line of show horses, I noticed a flaw in the tail of a quite famous horse. On closer examination, I found that it was a completely false tail. I quietly went on down the line in the rear-view exam and circled to the head end. I gave each animal a thorough exam, but when I came up to the particular horse in question, I politely asked the steward to have the animal removed from the arena.

The exhibitor immediately let out with a burst of epithets about me, so I went to the rear of the horse, gave the tail a quick yank, and waving my trophy returned and handed it to its owner. Without further action, he hurriedly made an exit with the rear end portion of the anatomy waving like a flag.

The crowd, sensing a clear victory on my part, gave forth with a cheering standing ovation. I, myself, was titillated over a little piece of tail.

THE ENEMA

ONE FINE MORNING A FEW YEARS AGO, I RECEIVED A phone call from a client informing me that his favorite quarter horse mare had produced a new foal. The problem, according to him, was that the foal was standing around with its tail in the air, attempting to defecate but was not able to get the job done. This is quite a common problem in newborn foals because of the consistence and glue stickiness of the meconium, especially in foals from mares that had been stalled or penned for some time before foaling. Horses on the open range feeding on lush spring grasses are seldom afflicted. Exercise is also a contributing factor.

Ranchers generally feel they can treat most maladies themselves, saving the expense of a veterinarian's call. They sometimes do this out of sheer necessity. In this case, a visit from me would have involved considerable expense; the trip alone would have involved eighty miles of travel one way. So I gave the rancher my standard advice. He should mix a tablespoon of detergent with one pint of water, borrow his wife's douche bag, and give the colt an enema. I told him to call me if the desirable results did not follow.

My client had used douche bags in previous treatments involving the bovine species of newborn, administering nutrients such as colostrum, electrolytes, and amino acid orally. In cows, the tube was inserted in the mouth and run down the esophagus, so that the liquid could be placed right in the stomach itself. In the equine species, a stomach tube has to be inserted in the nares, or nose, to more readily reach the esophageal opening, due to the anatomical difference of the extremely long palate in the horse.

My client had witnessed my douche bag treatment only in calves. And I had never given a second thought to the fact that he might not know the definition of an enema. Instead he had prepared the solution I had recommended and had gone out, pried the poor little colt's mouth open, and inserted the tube. Instead of getting the fluid down the esophagus, he had put it

DOCTORING CALVES IN THE CALF CHUTE.

down the trachea. The result was disastrous; he drowned the poor foal. The foal died within two hours, and the client was right back on the phone to me with the sad news.

I asked him if he attained any results from the enema he had given. "No," he said. "For all the good it did, I might as well have shoved it up his ass!"

Ever since that incident, I always make certain that the clients know the definition of enema and the proper route of administration.

JAPANESE QUARTER HORSES

IN TIMES PAST, LIVESTOCK WERE WORKED WITH HORSES. But the advancement of technology brought forth the all-terrain vehicle and the three-wheeler. In some instances, motorcycles are even used. If you ever want to put a genuine spook on your livestock, this is the best way to do it.

Motors also add quite a few new hazards to livestock production that salesmen of these products seldom mention. I've watched a few motorized roundups that make bull-riding look tame. One seldom gets the chance to see a cowboy spread-eagled in the air, then go breast stroking across the prairie all in one quick view at a rodeo. A good badger-holed cow range provides enough danger and excitement to nearly demand the charge of admission to see what is going to happen next.

First of all, there is the noise. An entire division of tanks plus a few helicopters and jets make less noise than an armada of "Japanese quarter horses" at a daylight rendezvous. The first leg isn't so bad. A three-wheeler doesn't tire out like a horse, and on flat land during the first circle, it might actually outperform a horse. After that, its performance diminishes . . . as does that of its rider. An analogy, my definition of alcoholic beverages as described by Shakespeare, might be applicable at this point: "Alcohol increases the desire but diminishes the performance!"

Second of all, an armada of jeeps, three-wheelers, four-wheel drive pickups, and horse trailer wings for corrals can't compare to four or five good cowboys on genuine horses when it comes to penning four or five hundred cattle in one bunch. There are always four or five old cows that have escaped at some time or another and know all the avenues for evading entrapment. Along with them, there are fifty to one hundred calves that have lost their mommies and are looking back over their shoulder to see where they last saw them. When one calf breaks back and five three-wheelers attempt to get around him, the entire herd makes an escape. Pandemonium ensues, and the air is polluted with carbon monoxide and blasphemy that would toxify and

85

embarrass the most uncouth of any society.

In any given roundup, after about five attempts at corralling, this veterinarian is already a half day late for other appointments. I know that all schedules have to be revised, but my humor is usually depleted by this time, and a migraine headache disturbs what little thoughtful ability I have left. I feel like the man who started out with nothing and still has most of it left over.

When the mechanical riders get about three-quarters of the cattle corralled, they turn loose a quarry of blue-heelers along the chute to help a skeleton crew start working the cattle. A second wave of dubious anxiety hits me about this time. All the experienced hands are out rescuing the remainder of the cattle. The man responsible for catching the head gets "faked out" nine of ten times. My blood pressure goes up fifty points, and I know that my heart will be good for many, many more years if I survive the ordeal.

We quit running around when a few more of the cattle are brought in with their tongues hanging out and milk squirting from bags. They trot by me on the way to the working pens. Ten "Japanese quarter horses" are parked and shut down. My heart has stopped fibrillating, and we get back to work.

Somewhere in the back of my mind, the words "efficient production" pop up. I try to instill a few subtle thoughts of constructive criticism in my client's mode of operation while doing my job. My migraine headache slowly evaporates, and I find serenity in the labor of love for my profession!

Anyone for a complete practice in veterinary medicine? It makes my day when I see one three-wheeler broken into separate parts as I leave the premises three hours later than planned.

SOBER UP CREEK

THINGS WEREN'T TOO EXCITING AROUND THE OLD COW
camp. Two weeks before, Jim and Jack had made a little foray
down to Fort Benton and picked up nine head of horses that had
been left by homesteaders who had moved out of the country.
Two of the horses were genuine ridge runners, but the boys had
managed to corral the bunch and had necked the worst bunch of
critters together. They had also head-and-tailed a young stud and
a semi-crippled, wire-cut gelding that couldn't outrun his shadow.
They headed the bunch up toward the headwaters of the Marias,
formed by the junction of the Cut Bank River, the Two Medicine
River, and Dupuyer Creek.

The winter had been easy. The horses had nourished
themselves on stored fat and lupine stalks and pods, and were
plump enough to sell to the fish hatchery horse buyer that had
the contract to supply meat for all the young fish the hatchery
had in the rearing ponds.

Jim and Jack split the money from the horse sale, and a couple
of days later, it started to burn in their pockets. Both men were
genuine bronc stompers and booze fighters. In their camp, the
booze had vanished, and they were running a little short on
coffee and tobacco. Via the moccasin telegraph, Jack, who had
enough feathers in his hat but passed most of the time as white
instead of Blackfeet Indian, found out about a Saturday dance in
Dupuyer, or Fat Back Creek, which is the English version of
Dupuyer's name.

The boys saddled up a couple of their top horses and headed
for the town of Dupuyer. Sometime that night, they ended up
about forty drinks below, having gotten into a couple of bouts of
fisticuffs. In fact, Jim had knocked his partner down when his
face got in the way during one of the fracases. The partner, Jack,
had been trying to separate Jim and a friend when a roundhouse
blow connected with the wrong man and left him stretched out
on the floor. I never heard anything more about the dance. They
found themselves sobering up the next morning on a little creek

about two miles from town. Hence the name Sober Up Creek.

Their story was told to me when my old friend Jimmy Sullivan accompanied me on a veterinary call. Jim had sworn off booze before going into matrimony at the request of his future spouse. He never did take another drink of hard liquor or liquor of any kind. He made up for it, though, in coffee consumption and Bull Durham hand-rolled cigarettes.

That particular call had been a very messy one, involving a caesarean section on a cow that had been in labor for nearly a week. The fetus was very odoriferous, and I saw Jimmy turn away and go through a few fits of the dry heaves. After I had finished the operation and was on my way home, he told me that his craving for a shot of whiskey was the worst he had experienced since the day he quit drinking.

Sober Up Creek is the location of another little tale I will relate. A little bridge over the stream was being inspected by a highway crew a few years ago, when, lo and behold, the crew found the body of a grizzly bear under the bridge. I'm not so wise as the fish and game guys, but I never did hear if they discovered the cause of his demise. I have two theories, however. The first is that he died of lead poisoning, and someone was too lazy to shovel. The second is that he consumed a huge meal of fermented grain that contained a very high level of alcohol, and made it all the way to Sober Up Creek before meeting his end from acute alcoholism.

THE SHEPHERD

WHEN LEWIS AND CLARK TRAVERSED THE BIG COUNTRY IN which I chose to practice, the area was blessed with wildlife. The explorers' description of endless herds of buffalo roaming the prairie has always made me wonder what it would have been like to be with them. In such historic days, river bottoms sheltered the deer and elk herds beyond count, so the animals were stalked and hunted by the Indians for food and clothing. Even Captain Lewis was a hunter, for the same reasons, and he suffered the first recorded hunting accident in Montana on his return down the Missouri River. After all the other dangers he had survived, one of his men mistook him for an elk and put a bullet through his rump, nearly killing him.

Lewis's encounters with grizzly bears, however, are classic histories of the ferocity of that animal. The audacity and fearlessness of the beast made the bear the nemesis of the Indians and white men alike. A wounded grizzly was worse yet, really living up to the bear's scientific name of *Ursus horribilis*. People and grizzly bears don't mix well, and the damage they have done to each other can fill many volumes.

I received a call one day to inspect a band of sheep for shipment to feedlots and markets in various parts of the United States. My itinerary took me to a sheep camp in the foothills of the great chain of the Rocky Mountains as they rise up out of the prairies to stand as majestic statues against the western sky. These peaks are the last great reservoir of wildlife as they have retreated to a safer and less accessible sanctuary. In the face of such wilderness, I often thought about taking a few days off for a hunting trip. But business and my duties as a veterinarian limited my chances of getting time for such things. It was nice to dream about, though, as I wound my way to the base of the mountains.

The wind picked up as I bounced along the narrowing trail that led me to Broadie Smith's camp that fall day. A few snow squalls were hitting the hills as I finally arrived at my destination. A sheep wagon stood beside a stockade that sheltered the animals during storms and strong winds. Two small sheep dogs came bouncing from under the wagon to meet me. The door of the wagon popped open, and a friendly voice beckoned me over for a visit and some coffee.

Broadhurst Smith was an immigrant from Ireland. He had worked for various outfits in his younger days, and through frugality and hard work had put together a band of his own. He wintered his sheep in the foothills and summered them back in the mountains. He was on his way out to the counting corrals to wean, ship, and pick up the bucks to start a new crop on the way for another year.

I couldn't keep my eyes off the man. His head was completely devoid of hair, with ugly scars running every way over his scalp and face. Even his hands and lower arms were knotty and red from recent wounds. One eye kept running from the lack of an eyelid to channel tears to their proper place. He looked pretty

THE CROSS THREE RANCH AND THE ROCKY MOUNTAIN FRONT.

rough to me, and I wondered whether or not I should venture to ask the reason for his appearance. I didn't want to embarrass him. I didn't have to wait.

He must have sensed my curiosity, and it wasn't long before he told me a tale that curled my hair. Here is his story:

"I trailed my sheep up the North Fork of Birch Creek to the forest permit for the summer. The grass was good, and I was camped on an open meadow. Everything was going fine until one night the dogs started raising hell and I could hear sheep running all over the place. I grabbed my gun and started down through the meadow. It was a bright moonlit night, and after I had gone about one hundred yards, I could make out the form of a huge bear eating on a sheep it had just killed.

"I walked a few more yards, and the bear must have heard me. It raised up on its hind legs and stood facing me, not thirty yards away. I pulled up my 30-30 and let him have it. The bear dropped, and I took him for dead, but just to be certain I pumped another shell into the chamber to give it another shot. I took good aim and pulled the trigger. There was only a click . . . that was it! The bear was on its feet and was on me before I could do another thing.

"I flew through the air and lit in a heap. I tried to protect myself by putting my hand over my head. It was lucky that I had lit face down, or I wouldn't have any face left. I could feel the bear's jaws clamping down on my skull and tearing off my hair and scalp. I wondered if it would ever stop. My only chance was to lay there and take it, hoping he would give up or be weakened by the shot he had taken. I knew I couldn't last very long. The bear finally quit, but I was hurt. It had bitten into my arms and back. I was bleeding, but conscious, and afraid to move for fear that he would attack again. I had heard many bear stories and knew I had better play dead.

"I don't know how long I lay there. It seemed like an eternity. I was afraid to move. I was still alive, but one movement and another attack would be the end of it for me. Finally I decided that I had to do something before I bled to death. I had surmised that I had been there over a half hour, and that the bear would be gone by now. I was wrong. The minute I tried to get up he was on me again, and the terrible crunching of those jaws on my body made me lose hope. I knew I couldn't last long.

"My last hope was that the bear was weakening. His bites were not as vicious. I wondered when the end would come. It finally did. Whether the dogs distracted him or he finally went away, I don't know. I laid there until daylight and knew that I had to do something. I half-crawled and staggered back to the tent. I was weak and bleeding. Patches of my head were ripped off. I found my gun. There were no shells in it. What a lesson I had learned. I needed help, but there was none closer than seven miles down the canyon."

No one will ever know how he made it. Broadie couldn't tell me himself. About noon that day he made it to a ranch at the foot of the mountains on his horse. More dead than alive, he was taken to the hospital one hundred miles away, and spent the next seventy-five days recuperating. The neighbors rounded up the sheep and another herder was put on the job. The bear was never found.

Broadie was back on the job with memories that would never leave. I inspected the sheep and headed for home amazed at the indomitable spirit of a man who had gone through living hell. I wasn't quite so anxious to go bear hunting after that.

THE BEAR WITH HALITOSIS

EXOTIC ANIMALS APPEARED AT OUR CLINIC FROM TIME TO time. We doctored everything from turtles to snakes, buffaloes to yaks, and pumas to bobcats . . . also parakeets, parrots, eagles, guinea hens, owls, and chickens. You name it, we made an honest attempt to treat whatever ills it might have. I've repaired ruptured yolk sacs on prize chickens and treated "Keel's" disease in water fowl. I always thought the name appropriate; when anyone inquired as to what it was, I usually replied it was when they "keeled over and died."

These events, when they occurred, made life a little more spicy, if variety is correctly referred to as the spice of life. One instance I recall particularly was when a man and woman stepped in our door and casually inquired if we worked on bears. "Not unless we have to, and you hold him down," I replied.

"No, I'm serious," the man said. "This old fellow is a family pet, but his teeth are bad. They need cleaning, and one or two need to be extracted."

Right then and there I was beginning to wonder which was the safest end of an animal to work on. I had been bitten by dogs, scratched and bitten by cats, kicked and shit on by horses and cows, gored by bulls, and run over by irate pigs. I knew both ends were treacherous at times. I have always been a great believer in the adage that ninety-nine percent of veterinary medicine is proper restraint.

Out of curiosity, I went out to make a visual examination of my newest patient. There he sat, eyeing me with wary suspicion and emitting a low growl. He was licking his drooling lips as if my hand and arm might make a tasty morsel in his daily cuisine. I was happy that he was confined within the strong bars of an iron cage. I didn't want him in my examination room. I recalled a couple of sayings, one about a bull in a china shop and the other a statement that I heard used in a debate in the state legislature about feeling much safer with a bear in my back yard than a plumber in my basement!

To get on with my story, after a little thought and consultation with the owners, I opened a can of dog food and uncoiled my trusty lariat. When the bear made the mistake of reaching through the bars for the food, I slipped the noose of the rope over his paw and threw on a trusty half-hitch for good measure. We pulled the entire leg out through the cage and I went to work administering intravenous anesthetic I commonly used on dogs and cats. This time, though, I used a 50 cubic centimeter syringe instead of the 10 cc type usually employed when anesthetizing canines. A tourniquet was applied to pop up the radial vein, and in a few seconds Mr. Bear succumbed to the netherworld of sedation.

After convincing myself that a proper level of sedation had been attained, we pulled the bear's head out, applied a good stout horse speculum between his jaws, and began the treatment. Talk about halitosis! The ole bruin had a case that would make anything else I've ever smelled smell like a rose. He had three rotten teeth and at least one-quarter inch of tartar on every tooth, plus a case of gingivitis that would make any human dentist do an Irish jig.

First we pulled the rotten molars with my equine dental equipment. Then we went to work with a small mallet and chisel on the tartar or plaque. By the time I had finished, my own sinuses and nasal cavity were nearly occluded from the odor. I made a resolution, then and there, that I would never miss another day of attending to my own dental needs.

Before the bear awoke, he was beginning to show signs of recovery. We made a pincushion of his hide with inoculations for distemper, hepatitis, leptospirosis, rabies, and a few others, including a goodly dose of a broad-spectrum antibiotic and a vermifuge.

The owners of the bear were extremely pleased and paid generously for all the services performed. They told me that every time the trainer put his head into the bear's mouth during a public show, they would think of me and remember how pleasant it was for him to be rid of his terrible halitosis. As for me, it took only a week to get sanitized!

PAT

ME AND PAT ON OUR ANNUAL SPRING OUTING IN GLACIER, BEFORE THE TOURISTS ARRIVE.

BEHIND EVERY SUCCESSFUL MAN IS A GOOD WOMAN. But to be the wife of a veterinarian takes more than just a good woman. It takes a saint.

I first met Pat when I returned from World War II and was attending the institution of higher learning, Montana State University in Bozeman. Our fraternity house held a spring party at a dude ranch in the valley of the Yellowstone near the park of the same name. Pat was there, too. A few sparks flew when I looked into her sparkling eyes. When I heard her infectious laughter and saw the beauty that went along with it, it turned into a genuine fireworks display.

I went away to school in Colorado and did not meet Pat again until I returned to start a veterinary practice in the great Golden Triangle of northwestern Montana. Again, the sparks and fireworks went off as I walked into a nightclub and found her sitting with a handsome gentleman.

It was not as if we were total strangers casually running into each other. Her brother and my brother had been classmates at college, and were sent overseas together. They went to England and then on to the invasion of North Africa. My brother was killed in the final days of the North African campaign. Her brother went on to the invasion of Italy and the horrors of that devastating campaign, and finally met his end. He was awarded the Congressional Medal of Honor posthumously, and today has his family name carried on at the National Guard unit in Great Falls.

95

After a whirlwind romance of skiing, rodeo, parties, homecomings, and trips in a brand new, sporty Ford convertible that I nicknamed "Ragtop," we were hooked up to the traces as a team for the long pull of living, loving, and sharing our life together.

It didn't take long to start a family when a careless Catholic and a passionate Protestant got together. Each fall for the next three years we were blessed with a beautiful kid and all the trials and tribulations of fatherhood, motherhood, and parenting. We finally found out what was causing this progeny increase, and after my sister brought a pair of twins into the world we slowed things down for a couple of years . . . after all, twin genes run in families! We tried to get a sister for our baby girl, but after two more boys we gave up and I took the matter of birth control into my own hands. So in case my daughter ever asks, this is the reason she has no baby sister.

The busy years came next. New and bigger houses, a new veterinary hospital, new this and new that until everything we had was new. New diapers, new shoes, and new clothes. Seventy to one hundred hours a week for me, and for Pat the twenty-four-hour day. As we look back, we wonder how she did it—meals around the clock, twenty-four-hour taxi service, daily laundry, daily janitorial service, t.l.c., doctoring, nursing, and all the other little things that go with motherhood.

We ended up with a royal flush of children. One lawyer, one paralegal, two veterinarians, two professional musicians, one teacher, one rancher. You ask how I got through the eighth grade, since I can't even add, but some of the kids have double careers. Hell, I can't even spell. When all five were in college at the same time, I kept telling everybody that Pat and I had "mal-tuition."

Today we have an empty nest except on special occasions. The family clan numbers over half a hundred with the progeny of my siblings. If we threw in Pat's side of the family, it would pass into three digits. Our family's so extensive anymore we can't say anything bad about anyone because we might be talking about a relative.

Times change, and today we are still loving, caring, and sharing. Sparks and fireworks still fly, especially when the traces and tugs on my side of the wagon show a little slack. We still share, but the ratio has changed. Pat has twenty drawers and I have two. She has twenty feet of clothes hangers; I have two. She has twenty pairs of shoes; I have two—one pair covered with manure that I can't wear in the house, and one pair of Ryan anteater specials that I can't wear out of the house.

Talk about great women. She is still the greatest. We share memories of annual ski trips with five kids in tow; of the annual quest in the mountains for the proper Christmas tree; of five stockings filled with goodies on Christmas Eve; of my yearly trips and our hamburger breakfasts; of spelunking adventures that drove guides insane; and of hip circles on high bars two hundred feet over the falls of the Yellowstone.

We haven't lacked excitement. My wife is an excellent artist and can paint much better than I can write. She liked me a lot more when I first told her that she was a better cook than my mother. I could go on and on, but words can never describe the part she has played in my life and the lives of others she has touched. How could I be so lucky?

Under The Chinook Arch

FORTY-THREE YEARS AGO I MOVED INTO MY PART OF Montana to practice veterinary medicine. I was the only veterinarian from Kalispell to the west, Havre to the east, and Great Falls to the south. An area larger than some states, this part of the country is often called "The Golden Triangle." The Canadian border lies to the north, the Rocky Mountains and the continental divide to the west, and the Missouri River to the south. The Bears Paw Mountains form the eastern boundary.

As southwesterly winds fall off the mountains, they warm 5.3 degrees Fahrenheit every thousand feet in descent. Doing so, they form a phenomenon I call the Chinook Arch. Clouds cloak the mountains, leading into a blue bank of clear sky for twenty to forty miles on the eastern slopes, and ending in a lenticular cloudy arch extending from north to south as far as the eye can see. It is a beautiful sight.

I commute in the area from my home to various ranches and would like to describe a typical trip that I have made for the past forty-some years:

I rise at 4:30 A.M. and gather the material necessary for a day of pregnancy diagnosis on a herd of 450 cattle. I hit the road south (I-15, also known as the Al-Can Highway) and go for about ten miles. On the way south, I do not meet or pass even one vehicle. I can see the lights of two antiballistic missile sites and the lights of two towns, Conrad and Brady. Two great planets loom in the sky—Venus in the east and Mars in the west. In between lie the belt of Orion and the brightest star in the heaven, Sirius. As I turn east at Brady, I can see the phosphorescent lights of a huge new Exxon anhydrous ammonia and fertilizer plant and a dim glow to the south of lights from one of Montana's largest cities, Great Falls.

The greatest sight of the journey, though, is the aurora borealis display of green, yellow, and red bars streaking across the northern skies. They seem to race one another to the eastern edge of the spectrum, then return to the west to start the undulating colors again. It is a sight that amazes me, and one I never tire of watching.

A few miles farther east, I cross Dead Indian Coulee on the Whoop-Up Trail, which stretches between Fort Benton on the Missouri River to the Canadian outpost of Fort McLeod in Alberta. Most of the trail has now been plowed under by the sons of the soil in one of the nation's greatest breadbaskets. Mile upon mile of strip farms loom in the headlights as I pass the alternating fields. I recall that, in 1806, Captain Meriwether Lewis described this country as black with great herds of buffalo. The buffalo were in rutting season and made a tremedous low roar all night long, Lewis wrote. He was on his way from the Marias River region to a rendezvous below the Great Falls of the Missouri after the only serious skirmish his corps of discovery had with the Blackfeet Indians.

I pass through the early morning, going sixty miles an hour. On one side are low-lying hills called the Knees. A few miles farther, I leave behind another hill called the Goosebill. The sun

THE OLD HOLY FAMILY MISSION ON THE TWO MEDICINE RIVER, ESTABLISHED 1886.

is rising in the east, and I am treated to a spectacular Charles M. Russell sunrise. The colors are gorgeous. The Bears Paw Mountains and Studhorse Butte are visible in the east. Square Butte, Round Butte, and the Highwood Mountains are to the south. Only Charlie Russell has captured the colors and topography of this domain in his famous paintings.

As I near Fort Benton, I can picture the artistry of Mr. Russell showing the Jerk Line horse caravan and a wagon train pulling away from Fort Benton on the Whoop-Up Trail. Here I take a short cut, and swarms of Hungarian partridges cross ahead of me in the early morning light. I slow down for numerous deer herds before dropping down to the valley of the convergence of the Marias, Teton, and Missouri rivers. I am again reminded of Montana's early history. Statues here commemorate the massacre of early settlers by a group of Indians and the dilemma of Lewis and Clark in determining the main branch of the Missouri River. An excerpt from Lewis's and Clark's journal describing a buffalo in camp makes me chuckle to myself.

I then join the main highway from Great Falls to Havre and, after climbing out of the river breaks, journey through the strips of wheat farms on my way to Big Sandy on the eastern foot of the Bears Paw Mountains. I finally meet a car and three huge cattle trucks before turning south at Big Sandy. I skirt the foothills through the old McNamara and Marlow Ranch, and pass by more deer, antelope, Hungarian partridges, sharptail grouse, sage grouse, soaring hawks, and golden eagles. I arrive at my destination 160 miles from home, ready for work. I pregnancy-test over four hundred head of cattle and return homeward under the Chinook Arch, a panorama of silver-lined clouds cloaking the massive and beautiful Rocky Mountain front as the sun sets.

As I approach my home, the arch extends all the way from Chief Mountain on the Canadian border to the Belt Mountains in the south. The arch covers a land once occupied by immense herds of dinosaurs whose fossil remains are evidence of a dynamic world. It covers a land that has been inhabited by ancient explorers from Asia, the descendants of these nomadic peoples known today as Native Americans. The land had felt the tread of later explorers Meriwether Lewis and William Clark and their corps of discovery. The fur traders and trappers followed, supplying the whims and fads of a shrinking world made smaller by better transportation. Then came the miners, searching for the stuff of elusive dreams, for gold and riches. The vast herds of cattle and sheep came next, replacing the vanished bison. The open range was in turn replaced by the plows of homesteaders who turned under the plains to make the breadbasket of the world. Their spades cut the sod to form the roofs and walls of homes, some of which are still visible today.

As I travel this country, I am reminded of its great resources. Oil and gas are found in the bowels of the earth under the arch. Coal lies under the uppermost layers, exposed in seams eroded by streams and rivers as they flow to the Arctic and Atlantic oceans. A living resource, the livestock industry still thrives. It is by far the most important and far-reaching facet of life in this rural region today. I am fortunate to have been a factor in its development and survival here.

Still the greatest resource of all is the people. To me, the people who live in this land are the greatest on earth. They say the good Lord passed out favors and brains on a square-mile basis; with a density of two to five people per section, it is easy to see the chances of endowment here.

It has been my pleasure to work, live, and love in this land for most of my life. Happiness is contagious, and I am thankful, too, for the endemic spreading of this condition. I sincerely thank all of those who have touched me. May God bless them all.

RIB'S POEM: DAILY CIRCLES

There are many things as lovely as a tree,
  A thousand we miss each day when spring goes on its
    yearly spree.
It's up in the morning around the hour of four,
  Give or take five because alarms are a bore.
No need to be exact because time is so fleeting;
  Be comfortable with just living and being.
A bit to eat, coffee to sip,
  A time to think, a time to dream a bit.
A time to warm old bones and enjoy a minute around the stove,
  Then into your boots and into your chaps, into your scotch
    cap and the insulated clothes.
Then it's out to the cold and breaking day, to see what is there.
  It snowed last night and the entire country has a new suit
    of pure white, fluffy underwear.
The horses are humped with their rumps to the north.
  A layer of white covers their backs.
I can see at a glance they don't like the weather
  As they wiggle their ears and shake their heads like they've
    been tickled by a feather,
Give a friendly nicker as the grain pan rattles, their heads sticking
    through the door.
  The feed boxes are filled; open the door, and they come
    clumping over the floor.
They are chomping the grain as they are haltered and tied,
  A curry and brush to rid the icicles from their frosty hide.
It's on with the saddle and a switching tail, a thumping of an
    ice-filled foot.
  The cinches are tightened, the bits are warmed, and coated
    with a layer of soot.
Then it's up and on and into the frosty dawn, to see what's
    happened in the eight hours since I've been gone.
The snow has stopped and the clouds are breaking;
  The moon is disappearing over the serrated peaks of the

great Rocky Mountains.
The clouds are tinged in a colored panorama as the sun's rays
    are broken into the colored spectrums, and I'm treated
    with a sight in the east.
    Damned pretty, to say the least.
I head for the herd through the still and soundless world,
    With the exception of the ripple of the river and the
    water's whirl.
I find the first calf, the cow has licked him dry. He is less than
    an hour old.
    He is shaky on his feet, but his instincts have taken hold.
    He's desperately searching for his life to unfold.
I ride on. Mother Nature in her near perfect design
    Has filled my world with copious signs.
A white-tailed doe with last year's fawns
    Has made a nocturnal search for some sappy twigs and left
        her tracks for the safety of the woods in the coming dawn.
The great horned owl with its round huge eye
    Swivel necks my progress as I slowly ride by.
A few cotton-tailed rabbits have hopped here and there,
    And a chipmunk has searched for a nut he buried somewhere.
The silence is broken by a pair of honkers in their morning calls.
    Their wings are thumping as they soar on by in the
    crisp spring air.
A coyote trail comes down from the rim;
    He is outlined on the opposite horizon when I finally
    catch a glimpse of him.
I find another pair. The newborn calf has found a faucet,
    and his gurgling sounds of contentment are similar to an
    old cowboy who likes his whiskey neat.
    Like the cowboy he is, still a little staggering on his feet.
It's on up the river where two cows have found their old
    nursery spot.
    They eye me with caution and with a shaky head and warning
    paw, urge me on by and bother them not.
To my right in a snaggy old tree

Are a bevy of sharptail grouse. Their clucking indicates they
are aware of me.
The wing prints on the new fallen snow indicate they've been
      dancing. I missed their drumming on the morning ride.
  Their prancing and strutting indicates spring has arrived.
I leave the valley and head up the trail.
    Labor pains have hit a cow; she's circling around to see what's
      under her tail.
The sun is now in full bloom. The mountains loom in the
      morning light;
  The omnipotent has presented a glorious sight.
A wandering badger in his nocturnal rounds
  Has left a trail of great brown mounds.
High overhead a golden eagle circles the big sky,
  Searching for game with his eagle eye.
It's back to the ranch with my morning report.
    The boss casually asks, "What's up, ole sport?"
"Nothing," I say. "Everything's normal. I think the good Lord
      pricked the Devil with his own fork."

APPENDIX: RIB'S WESTERN PERSONALITY TYPES

Booze Fighter—This is self-explanatory. It usually refers to the "spree" drinker or ranch hand who goes on one every time he hits town. He usually forgets to come home, or intentionally stays away. Money burns a hole in his pocket, and he usually doesn't quit until his finances are depleted or his credit is used up. He is usually smart and a good worker, and swears that he is on the wagon for good. He calls himself a periodic alcoholic, and the next time he hits town repeats the performance. His motto is, "The best way to get over a hangover is to postpone it."

Bum—This term is reserved for a particular person who has attached himself to a single facet of endeavor without any spectacular results. Bums come in various forms, shapes, and sizes without regard to sex, color, religion, or physique. In my day I have known "ski bums," "cowboy bums," "golf bums," "rodeo bums," or what have you. They usually know everything about the sport or endeavor they have become attached to. Usually they "caddy" up to some famous personage in order to be identified. They know absolutely nothing and care about nothing except that which has taken their fancy. Being a "bum" can take up an entire lifetime, and is usually boring to all except number one.

Gunsel—A term used to describe a person who doesn't quite come up to expectations, one lacking in common sense and who always seems to be in the wrong place at the wrong time, who can't think ahead and never knows quite what is going on. Other than that, he might be all right, especially to his own way of thinking.

Hormones Clanking—The same as being "in heat." Either sex is susceptible. This term has to do with the attraction to the opposite sex and manifests itself in many different ways, mainly in men who think they are God's gift to women. This clanking increases with alcohol consumption and probably follows the World War II adage, "Candy's dandy, but liquor is quicker."

I.Q. Lower Than a Snake's Belly in a Wagon Track—This phrase may indicate the first cousin to the gunsel, but it is usually reserved for a particular person with no comprehensive ability or, in other words, who's just plain dumb. It may also be a high school or college graduate who is allowed to matriculate because no one wanted him or her back. Usually his mode and way of life is "just like grandpappy used to do it."

Jesus Jumpers—Religious fanatics who go overboard. These people have ideas, and, as philosophers have always warned us, "Watch out for people with an idea. They will try to inflict it on you." This type of person is usually quite demonstrative in church, at political meetings, and at table grace.

Old Gonna—A term reserved for people who are always thinking ahead and are "gonna" do something to set the world on fire. They have big plans that never seem to materialize, and when one plan fails and fades away they are "gonna" do something about something else. They are promoters who never seem to promote. Usually they are looking back on failures, boredom, or whatever, and are "gonna" do something about it. I have several friends in this category and often wonder if I'm not one of the crowd. I'm always "gonna" quit smoking, lose weight, or things like that. I'm often "gonna" take up running to get in better shape.

APPENDIX

Round Asses—These are the people who like to ride horses and classify themselves as excellent riders or horsemen or cowboys, but who usually end up biting the dirt anytime anything unexpected arises. Again, the term is self-explanatory, and is like trying to put a rubber ball on a saddle and expecting it to be there at the end of the day without tying it on.

Sidewalk Cowboys—they always carry a gun with a lariat showing along with it in the back window of their four-wheel drive pickup. There even may be a blue heeler on the seat in the cab or in the box. They always wear a well-cared-for hat creased in the newest fad, and eighteen-inch boots with underslung heels. They make certain they come into town everyday to drink coffee or beer and stuff a pinch of snuff in their mouths as they get up to leave. They avoid all work, bad weather (except on hunting trips), and never walk. Cowboys and pilots don't walk. They are certain to ask all the ranchers if they need a hand. They are "all hat and no cattle."